Read to me:

Raising kids who love to Read

Bernice E. Cullinan

SCHOLASTIC INC.
New York Toronto London Auckland Sydney

Permissions:

From "Bedtime" by David L. Harrison. Copyright © David L. Harrison, used by permission of Boyds Mills Press.

From *Goodnight Moon* by Margaret Wise Brown. Copyright © 1947 by Harper and Row Publishers, Inc. Copyright renewed 1975 by Roberta Brown Rauch. All rights reserved. Reprinted by permission of HarperCollins Children's Books.

Photo Credits:

Cover photos: (Top to bottom) Copyright © G & M David de Lossy/Image Bank; Copyright © Dan Heringa/Image Bank; Copyright © Janeart Ltd/Image Bank; Copyright © Stephen Marks/Image Bank.

Interior photos: Page 5: © 1992 American Library Association/Mary Mewha. Page 19 © Reading is Fundamental, Inc. Used with permission. Page 35 © 1992 American Library Association/Connie Thompson. Page 39 © 1992 American Library Association/ Jennifer L. Derks. Page 49 © 1992 American Library Association. Page 65 © Reading is Fundamental, Inc. Used with permission. Page 81 © 1992 American Library Association/Lauren Koepsell. Page 101 © 1992 American Library Association/Kerry Blum. Page 116 © Reading is Fundamental, Inc. Used with permission. Page 134 © 1992 American Library Association.

ISBN 0-590-45206-1

Copyright © 1992 by Bernice E. Cullinan. All rights reserved. Published by Scholastic Inc.

Library of Congress Cataloging-in-Publication Data
Cullinan, Bernice E.
    Read to me : raising kids who love to read / Bernice E. Cullinan.
        p. cm.

ISBN 0-590-45206-1

    1. Children — Books and reading.   2. Reading — Parent participation.
I. Title.
Z1037.A1C85   1992
649'.58 — dc20   91-34324
                                                            CIP

12 11 10   5 6 7/9

Printed in the U.S.A.   **40**

First Scholastic printing, June 1992

To my daughter, Janie

Acknowledgements

I want to thank the families who have allowed me to tell their stories here. I thank them not only for their permission but for their devotion in handing down the magic of reading to their children. I also want to express my gratitude to Michelle Rapkin, who worked lovingly beside me as editor and friend.

Table of Contents

Introduction

Each year Gracie Peaslee would tell her kindergarten students in Pinellas Park, Florida, to bring from home the largest pair of socks their parents could find. And, because they were kindergartners and not twelfth graders, everyone of them complied.

Once all the socks were in, Miss Peaslee would sit her students around her and tell them, "Today we are going on a class trip. But first we must put on our special socks. However, we're not going to put them on the usual way. Today we're going to put them on *over* our shoes and sneakers."

Of course the children could hardly believe their ears. Nonetheless, with Miss Peaslee assisting, and with much pushing and pulling, they were all finally dressed with the socks over their shoes. The giggling class was then paraded outside to a nearby field

1

where they were encouraged to romp about to their hearts' content, then returned to the classroom.

Inside, Miss Peaslee told them to remove their socks, after which she held her own aloft for them to see. She pointed out all the tiny seeds that had attached themselves to the socks. "You've probably seen such things sticking to your clothes before but never knew they were seeds hitching a ride. And just to prove they are seeds, we're going to *plant* them."

She then passed out flowerpots to the children and told them to bury their socks in the dirt. This accomplished, the pots were placed on the windowsill and dutifully watered each day by the children until a wide assortment of weeds, grasses, and even flowers began to grow.

Gracie Peaslee's class project is a perfect example of how to raise not just a flower but a reader and writer as well. Young impressionable minds are very much like fuzzy socks. The wider and richer the fields of experience we bring them through, the more ideas and skills will stick to them and eventually grow.

Children whose parents have taken them to museums and libraries, and to visit relatives in faraway places, these children invariably have larger vocabularies and interest spans than do children who spend their days monotonously watching four hours of television in the same neighborhood day after day.

Competent readers and writers are no more born than athletes are. Not one player in the National Football League was born wanting to play football. That desire had to be planted by someone — usually a father or uncle, perhaps an older brother. And you can be sure there were little rubber footballs around his home as a child and he was taken to neighborhood playground scrimmages while still a youngster. In each instance, seeds were being planted that would someday blossom into a professional athlete.

So it is with competent readers and students. If you look at the childhoods of adults who have succeeded in school and life, more often than not you find they have been taken through fields of experience that enriched their minds. Most often they were read to — just as someone played catch with the athlete. An adult in their lives talked with them a lot, asking their opinions. They had library cards and some books on their bedroom shelves, drawing paper, crayons, and pencils. Quite simply, those are the tiny, inexpensive seeds that grow readers.

Dr. Bernice Cullinan brings a unique set of credentials to this wonderful collection of ideas for raising readers. She is, above all, a parent and grandparent. And to that she brings her added perspectives as a classroom teacher, college professor, educational researcher, and past president of the world's largest association of reading teachers. Quite simply, Bee Cullinan combines the common sense practicality of a parent with the research-based ideas of the professional teacher. Her activity and book suggestions are always on the mark and focused on parent and child *enjoying* the experience of print — not just enduring it. This is 180 degrees away from the drudgery of flash cards and worksheets.

Here are rich fields of literature for parent and child to wander in, filled with the seeds of wonder, creativity, and excitement that make learning what it is supposed to be — fun and successful.

— Jim Trelease
    author, *The New Read-Aloud Handbook*

3

Chapter 1:
Raising Readers

Raising children is one of the most important jobs you'll ever tackle. You didn't apply for the job, you don't get paid one cent to do it, it's a twenty-four-hour-a-day job, you don't get vacations from it, and it lasts for many years. The job — being a parent — has a great payoff.

Although you aren't paid in money, the rewards are tremendous. The rewards come from watching your children grow into loving, responsible, competent human beings. That's no small accomplishment! Our children are the hope of the future. We need to nurture them carefully. If you teach your children to love to read, you are handing down a special kind of magic to them — a gift that will enrich their lives as nothing else can do.

You take your job seriously. You make sure your child eats healthy food and has proper rest. You get sneakers that are the right size so the feet will grow straight. You buy the right kind of clothes to make sure your child stays warm. But what about your child's mind — are you feeding the imagination? Are you feeding that endless curiosity that causes children's minds to grow in a healthy way?

It seems as if you answer a hundred of your child's questions a day and you know you will continue to answer lots more. But you also know that your child needs to learn from other sources, too — and that includes books! Books contain an endless source of knowledge . . . and pleasure. When you go into a library or bookstore or see a book club offering, you see hundreds of books, and you want to make good choices. That's what this book is about — how you can help your child discover the wonderful world of books and become an enthusiastic lifelong reader. You'll discover some unexpected bonuses, too.

Your child will:

- *Do better in school*
- *Improve as a reader*
- *Enjoy a richer, fuller life*

These goals are not to be sneezed at; they're worth working for. You may say, "But I don't know how to teach my child to be a reader. That's the school's job." Certainly the school has a very important role to play and will spend many years developing reading skills, but you have the most important, most continuous, and most lasting influence on your child as a reader! The school needs you as a partner; your continued support over the years makes a lasting difference. School cannot do the job alone nor can school do it as well as it could with your help.

Some very simple things you do now have a big payoff in the years to come. For example, you can say, "Come here and look at this book I'm reading. It's about books I'm supposed to read to you. Let's see if we can find one that looks good to you." Letting your children know that you are interested in their books tells them that reading is important to you. Even more crucial, it tells them that *they* are important to you. Asking them to find books they like shows that you want them to enjoy reading; it tells them reading is not a chore, but something you are supposed to enjoy. It is the beginning of many happy hours spent sharing books.

How Children Learn Language

You are your children's first and most important teacher. You've already taught them one of the most complex and difficult skills imaginable — language. You taught your children to talk, to listen, and to understand language. You probably say, "Oh, but they learn that naturally." It's amazing to realize but if you do the same things you did to teach your children to talk, they will learn to read and write naturally, too. It is true: The very same conditions that help children learn to talk also help them learn other skills. Reading and writing, a part of language, can be learned in the very same way that children learned to talk. If we do the same things we did when our children were learning to talk, they can learn to read and to write with pretty much the same ease. Let's look at what we do when children learn to talk.

We say that a child learns to talk naturally. If you think about what you did to help your child learn to talk, you'll see that there were certain learning conditions present. For example, from the very moment your child was born, you surrounded her with language. You talked to her while you were feeding her. You talked to her while you were dressing her. You talked to her while you were bathing her. You never stopped talking! We literally drench children in words as we fill every waking moment with the sounds of our language. Even though you said, "Well I know she can't understand me," you kept on talking. Just as you surrounded her with talk, now we need to do the same with reading and writing.

Your child gradually attached meaning to some of the words she heard and began to try to say them. You were providing models, or giving her demonstrations of language. You showed your child what language is by demonstrating what it does. Your child learned that she could use language to get others to respond — to give her a hug or a drink of milk. Children learn that language gets things done that they want to accomplish. They find that language makes things happen. Since they want to be in charge of their world they will try it, too.

Your child tried to imitate some of your models by making sounds himself. When he first tried to use language his attempts didn't sound a whole lot like your model but you praised the effort. If he said "Wawa," you gave him a drink of water. You didn't scold him and say, "No, say water." When he first said "Mama" or "Dada" you really praised the attempt! You called your mother or the neighbor and had him say it again and again so that everybody could hear. We praise children for being close to right when they first try to say words. My granddaughter Trisha a little over a year old, just started saying "nank oo." We all pretend she says, "Thank you," and praise her effort.

If we do the same things to encourage reading and writing that we did to encourage learning to talk, children will learn to read and write just as "naturally" as they learned to talk. That means surrounding them with books (let them see that print is important), modeling reading by reading to them (show them how), and encouraging their attempts to read even when they make mistakes (praise their attempts).

The steps between knowing nothing about reading and becoming a fluent reader are similar to the steps between the child who makes "goo goo" sounds and one who speaks clearly. Every time I call my daughter, I ask, "What new words has Trisha learned?" The gradually earned and greatly praised process of learning to talk reflects what happens in reading.

Before we begin to talk about learning to read, we need to be clear about what we mean by "reading." Put simply, reading is getting meaning from print. There is really nothing simple about the process, however, but it makes it easier if you understand how it happens and where we are headed. It may seem logical to want to break reading down into small tasks, sounding out words and letters. But you did *not* do that with speaking. You did not have your child practice the /b/buh/ sound. You gave your child messages through words and sentences, and gradually your child began to create messages to send back to you. The emphasis is on the *meanings* of words. That's what makes sense to the child in speaking and reading. We have learned that we need to use whole words, not just sounds, to teach reading so that it makes sense to the child. Teachers now know the importance of keeping meaning whole in reading, writing, and listening, as well as speaking. Children learn better this way.

What Do We Mean by "Reading"?

Here are a few of the things your child learns to do as you make books and stories a vital part of life:

- *Hold a book right side up*
- *Turn to the front of the book to begin*
- *Turn pages at the appropriate time when the story is being read*
- *Point to words instead of pictures when reading*
- *Pick out a favorite book from a shelf of books*

These are the first steps in the process of learning to read. They are discussed in more detail in the age-related chapters that follow.

Our job of turning children into fluent readers is not completed once a child begins to read alone! In many ways, it's just beginning. We continue to support children's reading throughout their elementary school days by what we do and what we say. You will find tips to help you do that in this book.

The most important thing you can do to make your child a reader is to read aloud stories and poems — the more the better! Having books in the house for very young children makes them feel comfortable with books; books become their friends. Some books, such as toy books and pop-up books, become play things. Board books and plastic books get children used to the *feel* of books; they learn how to hold books, how to turn pages, and how to look at them for pleasure. The stories in books help children learn to read because they speak to their imagination in a special way; they encourage children to use their imagination and to play at make-believe and pretending. The ability to imagine, to see things in our minds that are not physically present, is an important part of reading. We use words to create pictures in our minds — a necessary part of learning to read.

Poems are fun for children because the words rhyme and are fun to say. Verses encourage children to bounce around while saying the words. The words match the rhythm of a child's movements; the rhythm underscores the words' meanings. Read the same poems and stories to your children over and over again; you'll soon hear familiar phrases fall trippingly from their tongues. Poems and stories give children words they never hear in ordinary conversation; children are word collectors — they grab hold of interesting new words and make them their own.

Writing Is Connected to Reading

Helping your child become a reader also involves writing, because reading and writing go hand in hand. Reading words that make sense and writing down words with children show them that these two activities are connected parts of the same process; two sides of the same coin. Writing shows a child that anything he says can be put into print; that talking, writing, and reading are all connected to meaning. There are lots of things in this area that you can do to make these connections visible. Here are a few:

Show your child a letter from Grandma. Point to the spot that says her name (surely Grandma used it). Write the message that she wants to tell Grandma. Let your child sign her name. Mail the letter. Maybe the return mail will bring a letter to her.

Give your child paper and markers so he can make pictures and write words and letters. Tape them onto the refrigerator to show off his work and your pride in it.

Write your shopping list for the grocery store in front of your child. Say the sounds of the words as you write them; exaggerate the sounds of the letters — *Mmmmm* as you write the letter M. Ask your child to show you where it says "milk," or "cornflakes." Let her copy words from the empty cartons. Ask her to help find the items at the grocery store.

When your child sees you reading and writing you are demonstrating what those skills can accomplish, and chances are your child will want to imitate you. Praise his attempts at reading and writing, the same way you praised his attempts to talk and walk. Let your child see that *you* get pleasure from reading. That's the best model of all.

Reading Is for All People, All Times, and All Places

Whatever your background, your reading level, or your occupation, there are books for you and your children. If you also speak Italian, read to them in Italian. If you also speak Spanish, read to them in Spanish. Because no matter what the language, we *must* read to our children.

Manuela Nita (nicknamed Vicky) was four years old when she came to America with her parents and little sister, Angela. Vicky, like her parents, spoke Romanian very well. That very September Vicky started kindergarten. She knew no English. About mid-October her teacher asked Vicky's parents to come to school for a conference when she could arrange for an interpreter. The teacher was concerned. She said, "Whenever Vicky wants to say something, she looks like she is going to speak but then she starts crying. I wonder if we're putting too much pressure on her." Her parents were concerned, too, but they did not see Vicky behaving this way at home; she chattered away each day telling them what happened at kindergarten. Since the family spoke only Romanian, that is the language Vicky heard at home.

However, Vicky and her parents watched TV a lot. Vicky's favorite programs were *Sesame Street* and *Mr. Rogers' Neighborhood.* Vicky's parents, like many new immigrants, were trying to learn English themselves. Vicky's father went to work every day although he had to take a job beneath his level as a skilled laborer; he had been an elevator repairman in Romania. His coworkers spoke English, however, and he began to pick up English rapidly.

Vicky spoke Romanian at home, listened to English at school, and watched television in English. Something must have started happening — English was beginning to make sense to Vicky. Six months later, in April, the teacher asked the parents to come to school for another conference. The teacher praised Vicky's school progress but said, "Vicky talks too much! She isn't quiet one moment! We can't shut her up!" Vicky's parents smiled, knowing that their little girl was feeling comfortable in a totally English-speaking environment.

Reading makes a difference in unexpected parts of our lives. We can use books to reassure a child who faces something that frightens him. One of my friends had to have tubes put in her son, Tommy's, ears as the result of repeated ear infections. Fear of the unknown made Tommy especially tense and uncooperative. After reading a story several times about Coco Bear who had tubes put in his ears, Tommy faced the simple procedure bravely.

Dorothy Butler, a bookstore owner in New Zealand, tells about her grandchild, Cushla, who was a multi-handicapped, chronically ill baby. Even though doctors told them that Cushla would have problems in school, her parents read books aloud to her to while away long hours in hospitals and doctors' offices. Despite her severe problems, at age six and a half Cushla was reading alone at a level far above her actual age. Her parents had made books and language a vital part of her life, and Cushla had fooled the doctors and learned, despite dire predictions that she would not.

Books can help you as a parent in many family situations. When a new baby is coming along, books that deal with that situation head on help a child express deep inner fears of being replaced or unloved when the newcomer arrives. Books can ease concerns about losing a tooth, having an operation, serving as a flower girl in a wedding, or facing parents' divorce. There is a backward and forward flow between books and what happens in real life. Children use real life experiences to help them understand books and books help them to understand real life.

We never know exactly what is going to appeal to a child so don't be too selective in choosing books. If your child loves toy trucks, try to find books about trucks. If he is interested in the stars, find some books on astronomy or sky watching. If she wants to be an astronaut, get her books about astronauts and space travel.

Telling stories to children is important, too. After all, it is the stories in books that make them so appealing to a child. We have an instant audience when we say, "Let me tell you about when I was a little girl."

My son said, "Mommy, tell me about the olden days when they had covered wagons and pioneers when you were a little girl." Stories about the good old days give children a sense of their family heritage. Do you remember some of the stories your parents or relatives told you? Isn't it fun to hear the one about how Aunt Emily nibbled like a mouse to eat chunks of icing off the pineapple upside-down cake while the rest of the family was out in the barn milking the cows?

Do you remember stories that you loved hearing as a child? Tell them to your children. You can edit out parts they might not understand — or parts you don't want them to understand! I told many stories about my little sister in which I took liberties to add to her misbehavior; Aunt Doty stories were ones my children asked for repeatedly. The stories you tell become part of your child's storehouse of experiences; they give him a wealth of understanding to face new experiences.

How to Use This Book

This book, *Read to Me*, is divided into three major sections. The first section (Chapters 1 and 2) shows that when children learn to read it is similar to the way they learn to talk. Reading and writing are part of language learning; if we do many of the same things for reading and writing that we did when they were learning to talk, children learn to read and write just as naturally as they learned to talk. This section explains how reading *to* children teaches them new words and shows them what reading is supposed to sound like. It states that in order for children to learn to read, they need to have someone read aloud to them. In this section you learn that reading is defined as getting meaning from print. You also find some things you can do to incorporate reading as a part of your family life. The strong connections between reading and writing are first explored here; they are extended in later sections.

The second section (Chapters 3 and 4) is packed with practical hands-on ideas. Because you are a busy parent, you need to find information quickly. Feel free to turn to those pages first to pick up some pointers on surrounding children with books and developing a love of reading. These chapters show exactly how to get started to make books available and appealing. The chapters contain numerous tips; they come from busy parents who know how to make reading a vital part of their child's life.

Section three (Chapters 5 through 9) is divided by age groups. In these age-related chapters you find features to explain what reading and writing looks like for each developmental stage. The chapters begin with a list of things children do as they relate to reading and writing activities. Each chapter features a child of that age to show how reading and writing fits into daily life. The chapters cite topics that most children are interested in, give specific reading tips for each age, and provide a list of age-appropriate books. The annotated lists contain books too good to miss at each age level. Turn to the chapter that applies to your child now. This is a self-help book intended to make life easier for you. It's time to get on with the fun that raising readers brings. Once started, it's a journey you never want to end.

In this book we suggest activities that lead children to read and ways to keep them reading. General tips appropriate for any age child appear in Chapter 4; activities that work best for a specific age group appear in the age-related chapters. For example, you find "You read to me and I'll read to you" in the chapter for beginning readers. The suggestion to have your child "Read one character's speaking parts" appears for older children who are well along their way in knowing how to read.

The special feature, "Did You Know . . ." contains all kinds of interesting bits and pieces of information related to children's reading and writing. The bits and pieces of information often relate to the effects of children's home activities on their school learning. For example, did you know that children will hurry to read a book they have seen dramatized on TV? You might think they would not be interested since they already know the story; but that seems to egg them on. Or did you know that reading series books helps children read better? Research shows that knowing a character and what you might expect in a story helps children read faster and more fluently. Did you know that the added reading practice from reading anything on their own makes children better readers? But that's what this book is about.

You're on your way! You have decided that you want to make reading important to your child. You know that you have taught her an important part of the language process and that you can take more steps to send her along her way to success. You bought this book and you're ready to go! You'll find it to be one of the most rewarding experiences of your life. When we plant flowers, we must sometimes disturb the earth. The blossoms we reap are worth the effort. Enjoy the planting.

Chapter 2:
Why Reading
to Your Child
Matters

One of my young neighbors with children ages eight, six, and four years old, said, "Thank goodness Brendan is reading by himself now so I don't have to read to him anymore." My neighbor is wrong about that! Even though eight-year-old Brendan can read, he still needs to have his mother read to him. When he sits close to her as she reads, he is reassured that he's still important to her even though younger siblings have invaded his space. He uses what he hears to make sense of his world and to understand what is happening around him. Books become a jumping-off place for Brendan and his mother to talk about real life experiences and to clarify questions. He sees the values of courage, honesty, and loyalty played out in stories and recognizes that he can live true to these values. When he shares stories with his family, he builds memories about the warmth and joy in his early life that will come back to him long after the memory of the story is gone. He also hears what reading sounds like when it is done by an adult. He carries the echo of that sound in his ear as he learns to read alone.

Brendan gets practice and develops confidence in himself by reading to his parents and to his younger brother and sister. But he still needs to hear stories read aloud to him, too. When he reads to others, he begins to see himself as a reader; he is doing what readers do. His growing independence in reading alone is strengthened by the praise he receives from his listeners.

No matter how much your child reads alone, however, it's still important for you to read aloud to him. There is more to reading than just saying words; reading aloud is a social event. Your child learns more than just stories; he learns about life, his family, and his place in the world. We tend to talk about a story while reading and continue to talk about it long after the reading is over. We relate events from the story to everyday life, saying, for example, "Today is just like Alexander's terrible, horrible, no good, very bad day," or "You're just like the little engine that could — you're saying 'I think I can, I think I can.' " Remember the models and demonstrations you gave your child to learn to talk. He needs models for reading, too. That's what you're giving him when you read stories aloud.

At my local library, I heard a mother ask the librarian, "Do you read aloud to the children during story hour?" When the librarian answered yes, the mother said, "Good. Then I don't have to!" Wrong! Even if the librarian reads aloud during story hour, it is still important for you to read to your child at home. The once-a-week or once-a-month library reading is only a drop in the bucket of what a child needs.

Hearing a story in a group at a library cannot compare to hearing a story read aloud by your own mother or father at home. The experiences are totally different. When *you* read to your children you are teaching them much more than just the material they are reading. You are telling them, "You are important to me, you are safe and secure, I will always protect you." You are saying, "We do things together as a family that are fun, wholesome, and worthwhile. We spend time with you because we care about you." All children need to hear these messages; reading together is a good way to tell them. Reading aloud establishes a close loving bond between a parent and a child that can be forged in no better way.

"The Reading Mother" points to the heart of the matter of reading to a child:

> You may have tangible wealth untold:
> Caskets of jewels and coffers of gold.
> Richer than I you can never be —
> I had a Mother who read to me.
> Strickland Gillilan

Children can understand more sophisticated and complicated books that are read to them than the books they can read alone. Until they're ten or twelve years old, children are better at listening than they are at reading. Around the time a child reaches junior high school, his or her reading ability catches up with listening ability. But until then, children are better listeners than readers. Therefore, you can choose books for reading aloud that are a bit above their reading level. You can read more complex books to them than those they can read alone; if they don't understand something, you are right there to explain it. By doing this, you encourage them to read books that stretch their reading skills.

A child is not likely to understand a word in reading that she has never heard. Understanding new words in spoken language comes before understanding them while reading. If a child has never heard the word "earthquake" she is not likely to recognize it or understand what it means when she faces it in a book. She certainly will not use it in her writing. But she will learn the meaning of the word from hearing you read about it and talk about it. Children build a storehouse of words from hearing books read aloud; they draw upon these words and their meanings when they read and write on their own. Choose books above their reading level when reading aloud; you'll be expanding their vocabularies.

Reading Aloud

- *Is fun*
- *Opens doors*
- *Builds the desire to read*
- *Gives educational advantage*
- *Becomes part of family heritage*

- *Establishes bonds of love*
- *Develops ability to read alone*

Reading aloud is fun because the stories themselves are fun — not only for your child listener but for you, the adult reader. Authors tell me that they think about the adults who read their stories to young children when they are writing them; they put in little jokes or subtle comments for the adults to appreciate. Outstanding illustrators consistently add detail that calls for repeated viewing of their art. You and your child find new things to talk about in the story and illustrations each time you reread a book. This is an unexpected pleasure of reading aloud: It's fun for you as well as your child. There are delayed bonuses, too, which are discussed later, but you'll be surprised to discover how much you will like the books yourself.

Another reason reading aloud is fun is the remarkably high quality of the books you read. Today children's books are more beautiful, more imaginative, more fun-filled than ever before. One of my neighbors explained, "I feel like a whole new world has opened up to me. I haven't even looked at kids' books since I was a child and I didn't pay much attention to them then. The only ones I read were Nancy Drew. I had no idea there were so many different kinds available — and they're beautiful!"

In some make-believe storybooks, spiders weave words into webs, pigs talk, and frogs play tricks on toads. The world's finest artists, writers, and poets contribute to children's books: the result — beautiful books. Some of the very best writing today can be found in children's books.

You make reading aloud more fun if, as you read, you speak in the voice of the characters. For *Goldilocks and the Three Bears*, use Papa Bear's gruff growly voice, Mama Bear's middle-sized voice, and Baby Bear's squeaky tiny voice. Even more fun, play-act the story with everybody taking parts. Children are always ready to act out or playact the parts of favorite stories. The first time you act out a story, assign parts that are fitting; that is, Dad could be Papa Bear, Mom could be Mama Bear, and the child, Baby Bear. After you've done it this way a few times, reverse the roles so that your child plays the Papa Bear. The whole game gets even more hilarious as you mix up the roles.

Read books in a tone that conveys their meaning. If a book is deliciously funny or silly, read it in a silly voice. If it's somber and sad, read it aloud in a serious voice. Give an appropriate voice to each character and read their words in that voice. Most of all, have fun while you read, and share the fun with your child.

Reading aloud to your child opens doors to worlds unknown. You open doors for your children by teaching them about their world. You can go to places you could never go in real life through books you read together. You also open doors for children by sharing the values — honesty, loyalty, courage — conveyed in books. But the most important value, that of reading itself, helps to make us human by allowing us to see the world from inside the skin of another person.

Reading aloud is one of the most useful secrets you'll ever find for being a parent: It soothes a sick child, calms a fearful one, and eases a fretful one into sleep. More importantly, reading aloud gives your child a gift of loving to read that stays with her always.

Reading aloud builds the desire to read. Children learn that exciting stories come from books and that reading is worth the effort. When we read children's stories as adults, they allow us to get in touch with the child still alive inside us. Both parents and children enjoy the imaginative stories, engaging illustrations, and lilting language found in today's children's books.

Reading to your child provides a valuable educational advantage; there's no better way to achieve it. Children who are read to do far better in school than those who are not read to. Children are sponges. They soak up everything they see and hear. When they hear stories they love they remember endless detail and learn things we are not even aware they are learning.

One important reason reading aloud gives children an educational advantage is what they automatically pick up about written language as they listen. Written language is not the same as spoken language. We use different words, different kinds of sentences, and different punctuation to express meaning. Children notice all these things as you read aloud, especially if they sit beside you and can see the page as you read. What they see and hear makes written language easier for them to understand as they read alone.

Reading aloud becomes part of your family heritage. If you read to your children, they will read to theirs. It's as simple as that. Children learn more than just words from living with us. They learn what we value, too. They learn more from what we do than from what we say. The things they learn become lasting memories. If you make books an important part of your life, children will remember the books, the stories, and the warm cozy times you spent sharing them. When they grow up, they will share the same things with their children. One day, my daughter Janie said, "Mom, when you read to us I just took it for granted. Now that I have my own children, I find that I'm doing the same thing. It's sort of like handing down the magic." We are handing down the magic of reading, imagination, and thinking when we pass on our love of books. It's a torch passed from one generation to the next.

Reading aloud establishes bonds of love. The actual content of a book may not be as important to your child as the feeling of coziness or sharing a special time with you. When a child and a parent share memorable experiences with a book, a certain feeling, called bonding, takes place. Bonding unites people. Sharing books and stories creates bonds that stay with us forever.

Remember how you still like the special food that your mom fixed when you were sick? Chicken soup is the magic medicine for some people, but for me it's cinnamon bits made from leftover scraps of pie crusts. My mother baked pies and always sprinkled cinnamon and sugar to bake on leftover scraps of the pie dough. Cinnamon tidbits bring a sense of warmth and well-being to me even now. Your children will always remember the special things that you give them when they are young. Books should be among their childhood memories. If they have those warm memories of cuddling with a parent and a good story, they associate those happy feelings with reading as they strike out to read alone. The feelings remain long after the stories are forgotten.

Children continually try to make sense of their world; they search for patterns to explain the way things work. They want to understand what happens to them, and they use language as their most powerful tool for organizing what they know. Some people call children "meaning makers"; they make sense of their world through language, and that is what they remember. Knowing and feeling are bound together in a child's mind. David Harrison poetically expresses the double edge of meaning in a child's request for a bedtime story. It doesn't really matter which story we read.

> "Read me a story,
>   Please read me to sleep."
> "But what kind of story, my dear?"
> "Read any story
>   And I'll go to sleep,
>   As long as I know you are near."

Reading aloud contributes to a child's ability to read alone. This happens naturally for many children who sit on a parent's lap to listen and to watch the reader's finger move across the page pointing to the words as they are read. Gradually, over time, children make connections between the sounds of words and the squiggles on the page. You don't need to start out by giving your child flash cards and isolated letters of the alphabet! You do, however, need to answer a child's questions. Tell him the names of the letters when he asks. Ask him to find words on the page that start with the same letter. Show him how to write his name. Put his name on the refrigerator with magnetic letters. Put it on his boots. A child's name holds immense fascination; it's probably the first recognizable word a child will write. The second message a child writes is often, "I luv u." What parent can resist that message?

All you need is the right book and time to share it with your child. That's what this book is about — sharing books, finding the right books, and making them important in your child's life.

Reading Alone

- *Expands a child's world*
- *Develops independence*
- *Stirs the imagination*

- *Establishes a lifelong reading habit*
- *Develops vocabulary*
- *Develops understanding of other people*

Reading alone expands a child's world. He can be transported to other times and other places through reading. He can see what it was like to come across the ocean on the *Mayflower* or to live during the early settlement of Plimouth Plantation in North America. History textbooks give facts, but historical stories have the power to make us feel as if we are living in a pioneer settlement. Through reading, your child can imagine life in the future or on a distant planet. Books help us consider the impossible and realize the many choices we have in life. They build a sense of wonder.

Reading allows us to live more lives than the one we have. We can face fear and loneliness without leaving the safety of our home. We can sail around the world without fear of shipwreck, or suffer blindness without loss of sight, while still probing the emotions of the moment. We can rehearse experiences we might someday have: We can find a friend or lose one, or climb a mountain in the Himalayas. Books cannot replace real life experience but they do help us decide which experiences are worth having.

Reading alone develops a child's independence. One of our goals as parents is to help children do things on their own. Reading alone helps a child to become independent as a learner. She can search for facts alone, entertain herself alone, and expand her horizons alone — if she reads. Reading paves the way on the road to independence.

Reading is one of the most liberating things we can do. In fact, before the Civil War, slave owners were so aware of the liberating power of reading that slaves were not allowed to learn how to read. Reading made them unfit for slavery. Frederick Douglass, a black leader in the Civil War period, learned to read in secret and passed on his secret to many others. Reading became the way to freedom; it still is.

Children sometimes act as if they want to be entertained all the time. They need to have friends around, or have the TV on, or be in the thick of some activity. Children who learn to read alone and love it can entertain themselves; they spend time alone happily. They are the ones who curl up with a book. Readers seem to have a good sense of themselves. They are comfortable with themselves and enjoy being quiet and reading. This type of independence will serve them well their whole life long.

Reading stirs the imagination — that ability to make believe and to imagine things that do not yet exist. The most intricate bridge could never have been built unless someone had imagined it first. Reading helps to create scenes in our minds that we could never see without vivid words. We may go to encyclopedias for facts but we go to stories for truth. Reading leaves us wondering about what is real and what is make-believe. Wonder is part of the magic that pulls us to stories time and again.

Reading alone establishes reading as a lifelong habit. It also makes children better readers because they get good at what they practice a lot. For example, if you practice playing the piano a lot, you get better at it. As you get better, you are willing to practice more. The more you practice, the better you get. And it becomes more fun. In reading, like so many other things, practice makes perfect. I call it a SUCCESS CYCLE. It is a cycle we want to get children into as readers. The more you read, the better you read. The better you read, the more you enjoy it. The more you

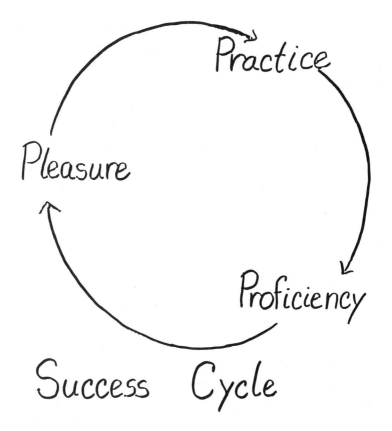

enjoy it, the more you want to read. Reading independently improves reading fluency — that ability to read fast and understand what we read.

Reading increases a child's vocabulary. The more words a child knows, the better she will be able to read. Through reading, children discover the meanings of many words that they would never come across in ordinary talk simply because people use words in books they don't use in speaking. For example, a book will state "she replied," but you seldom hear anyone say that.

Children learn the meanings of written words (language) by hearing them read and by reading them. The context, words surrounding the new word, often provides its meaning. It's not surprising: If you want to find out how well a child reads, find out how many words he knows. Knowing what words mean is a big help, in fact, a requirement, for knowing how to read them. It works both ways. We need to know a word before we can read it, but reading helps us learn the new word. Understanding what we read is fed by understanding what we hear.

Reading helps us to understand other people, their customs, and their cultures. We can walk in another's shoes and feel what it's like to live inside another's skin when we read something written from their point of view. We can understand life in historical times when we experience it through an historical novel.

Good writers describe people and situations so vividly we think we are there as we read. For example, we shiver from the icy blasts of wind as we read about the Little Match Girl and we feel isolation and rejection as we read about the Ugly Duckling.

When Homer Price cannot turn off a doughnut machine, we laugh but feel sympathy for him as he tries to find a place to put all the blasted doughnuts that keep popping out of the machine. We feel a bond of compassion as we see through another's eyes and read their words. Books help us realize that everyone shares feelings of sorrow, joy, confusion, and loneliness.

Reading alone brings untold advantages to children. And reading alone doesn't need to wait until children learn how to read by themselves. Toddlers spend endless amounts of time looking at picture books, chewing on board books with lively illustrations, and carrying cloth books to bed with them. They like to take plastic bathtub books into the tub. Preschoolers play with pop-up books until they wear them out or tear them up into pieces. All children can read wordless books — in any language! They can also "read" most picture books from the pictures alone.

As children learn to read on their own, the types of books that appeal to them change. Five and six year olds read and reread alphabet books and counting books. Beginning readers pore over easy-to-read books until they can master them. When they move beyond the easy-to-read books, children want chapter books in which they can read one episode or one brief chapter without tiring. They explore riddle and joke books to discover that books are really fun. Many readers move to books in a series in which the same character meets one obstacle after another. Boys often move onto science fiction while girls frequently prefer realistic or romantic novels. Whatever their taste, there are books to please every reader. Our job is to find the best books to establish the reading habit. The reading habit, a seed planted early, takes deep root. Nourish the seedling once it starts to grow, but the most important step is to get it planted. The flowers come later.

Chapter 3:
Getting Started

You may be like my daughter, Janie, who doesn't have a minute to call her own, and say you don't have time to add one more thing to your life. There's always something that must be done. But you've already started! You are reading this book! If you stick with the idea of raising readers, you'll have more free time in the future while your children are happily absorbed in a book. There are some things you're already doing to instill the reading habit, so capitalize on them. You have the desire to make your child a reader — and that's the most important part. The rest is simple.

It is never too early to start. But it's never too late, either. You don't need to read this entire book right now. If your child is seven or eight years old, turn to the chapter on seven and eight year olds. There you'll find suggestions about books to share and ways to share them. There are tips for busy parents that give at a glance, good ideas to put into immediate practice. Even if you are in an ideal situation, you wouldn't want to do everything suggested here. But you can do one thing. Flip through this book until you spot one good idea and try that. No matter what age your child is, the time to start is now. You can't begin too soon, so start today.

Ideas for Getting Started

1. *Keep books handy.* A stack of old favorites in a basket beside a big easy chair makes them convenient to grab at those moments a new activity is needed. Books on the bedside table show that reading is a natural part of the bedtime routine. A home library need not be expensive. With the low cost of paperbacks, you can have several for less than you pay for one breakable toy. Library cards are free. Trips to the library are an adventure and can bring in a new supply each week.

2. *Choose books your child likes.* You will pay no more money for a really good book that your child will want to read time and again than you will pay for an uninteresting book that doesn't hold your child's attention. This book helps to find those good books that children want to hear over and over.

3. *Set a special time for reading.* I always read to my children at bedtime but there was one other time that worked well, too. It was that fussy time just before dinner when we were waiting for Dad to come

home. The children were tired and hungry but I wanted them to wait to eat with their father, so I distracted them with a book. I would get all three of them on my lap, one on each leg and one in the middle, and prop a big picture book right in front of us all. It soothed restless children and changed fussy time into happy time. I know one mother who reads to her child at breakfast; it works if you are awake enough to see the page.

4. *Read at bedtime.* Reading at bedtime works wonders. When children are overly tired and bouncing off the wall, read them a story. Just start with a short poem or two. The magic of the words and the sound of your soothing voice calms down even the most energetic kid. Pick a time that works for you; even better would be three or four times a day!

5. *Don't panic if you miss a day.* There are always interruptions to schedules in a busy family. Just pick up again when the interruption is past. It takes time to get into a new routine. Good habits are worth working for and anything of lasting value takes work. In this case, however, the work is wrapped in pleasure and has long-term payoffs.

6. *Read 15 minutes.* Thirty minutes is better. Savor the time to get through a story and to talk about it. Busy parents are ones who get things done. When you establish book time on a regular schedule, your child won't let you forget it.

7. *Talk about the story as you read.* If the story is set in the city, talk about how the pictures of buildings in the book look like buildings in your town. If there is a grandpa in the story, mention how he is just like their grandfather. If there are things that your child doesn't understand, explain as you read.

The talk surrounding a book is important, too.

8. *Get others in on the reading act.* Make sure both parents take a turn at reading. If you are a single parent, ask the baby-sitter or child-care provider to read as part of each day. Big brothers and sisters join in by reading to younger ones while you are busy folding clothes or fixing dinner. Grandparents, aunts, and uncles make good readers, too. Your child needs to see that everybody gets pleasure from reading. This list of requirements for grandparents appeared in the local paper:

GRANDMOTHER	GRANDFATHER
Bakes cookies	Takes me fishing
Brings gifts	Loves TV sports
Hugs and kisses me	Has a great lap
Never rushes me	Never agrees with Grandma
Reads to me	Tells me stories

Chapter 4: Tips for Busy Parents

The care and feeding of readers is not an overwhelming task. All you need is a little creativity to take advantage of opportunities to put books in front of your children. Kids have busy schedules, too, so sprinkle books around them wherever they are. If they see you chuckling over a new book, they'll want to know what it's about. This chapter is divided into three sections: 1) general activities for every day, 2) activities related to television, and 3) activities for special times.

General Activities for Every Day

If you have ever gone on a diet and starved yourself for a period of time, you lost weight. But as soon as you went back to your regular eating pattern, you went right back up to the weight you were. The same is true for books in the home: If you make books central to your life for two weeks and then forget about them, your children will fall into their old ways. If you try to do just one thing — and do it regularly — it will work. The ideas here are ones you can incorporate into your daily-life schedule without a lot of bother; they are ones you can keep on using. They have worked for other families and they'll work for you, too.

1. *Put books in places your child will be.* Availability is the name of the game. If books are beside the toy box, train set, dollhouse, or pet's cage, they are more likely to be picked up. Keep books in the car or van. Put a treehouse mystery book in a real or pretend treehouse. Put children's cookbooks in the kitchen. Keep bedtime stories and poetry books beside the bed.

2. *Carry books along.* When you go to the dentist, the doctor's office, the health clinic, or places you may have to wait, have a book handy. Reading a story or a poem is a magical way to soothe a fretful child. Reading a poem from *Sing a Song of Popcorn*, a collection of verse, helps a child forget that he's feeling bad.

3. *Put books beside the bathtub.* Our son-in-law is a bathtub soaker-reader and our grandson has imitated his model. Our grandson has already passed through the plastic bathtub-books stage so now his mother keeps paperbacks stacked beside the tub. In case one gets a little damp, it's easy to dry it out. Soaking in the tub with a good book is a good habit to develop.

4. *Keep books and magazines in your child's room*. When children are "grounded" and sent to their room, they need to find interesting things to do there. When they spend time in their room, they are free to read. They will choose reading more often if books and magazines are there. There are over 150 magazines for children. A short list appears in the Appendix. Look for *Highlights for Children, Cricket,* or *Ranger Rick* for general interest columns, good stories and poems, word play, and articles about nature. A new supply of reading material addressed directly to your child arrives once a month with a magazine subscription.

5. *Have your child help with the grocery list*. Make out your list of needed items and assign part of the list to your child. One day I ran into Margot Cohen, a former student from NYU, standing near the checkout counter at the grocery store. As we chatted, her two children brought grocery items to put into her cart. Each time, she would show them the next item on the list and they would hurry off to find it. I congratulated her on teaching her children to read and she said, "Oh, they are saving me lots of steps, too."

Everybody who is alive is busy, especially people with children. But there are little windows of time when you can get your child to read alongside other activities.

6. *Read recipes*. All reading doesn't happen in books. When you're cooking something special, ask your child to read the ingredients to you. Many books have recipes in them. For example, see Sandra Sanders' *Easy Cooking for Kids* (Scholastic, 1979).

7. *Read road signs*. While you're driving, ask your

child to read the Stop signs, Yield, One Way, and street signs.

8. *Get taped recordings of books.* Many books have an audiocassette tape sold as part of a package. Professional performers or authors read the books in a dramatic way. If you don't have time to read to your child, let someone else do it. None of us has time to read as much as we would like but that is no reason our children should be denied this pleasure.

Activities Related to Television

During the several years that my daughter, Janie, was a single parent with two children, she had a full-time job, not enough money, baby-sitter problems, meals to cook, laundry to do, and a house to keep clean. One day I said to her, "Well, I hope you're *still* reading to my grandchildren." Janie turned on me like a tiger cornered in a cage and let out some of the silent frustration built up in her. She said, "Mom, are you crazy? I get up at six o'clock, throw a load of dirty clothes in the washer, fix breakfast, pack lunches, get the kids dressed, take them to the baby-sitter, and drive to work. When I come home, I pick up the kids, stop at the grocery store, fix supper, supervise homework, fold laundry, eat with the kids, and try to straighten up the house. When I get the kids into bed, I fall asleep exhausted beside them. I don't have the energy to read to them even if I could keep my eyes open! Who do you think I am — Super Woman?"

Janie frequently used TV as a baby-sitter so she

could get chores done, meals prepared, or just col-
lapse like a zombie. I felt compassion for her as I do
for other single parents and working parents, but
when things were a bit calmer I mentioned a few
things she could do to see that books and reading
were an important part of Kali and Jason's lives. How
can busy parents use television wisely?

1. *Watch TV shows based on children's books.*
Television is part of life so make the best of it; use
it to accomplish your goal of making your child a
reader. Many television programs encourage reading. When your child watches *Reading Rainbow,
Long Ago and Far Away*, or an Afterschool Special,
get the book featured on TV from a bookstore or library. Children willingly read stories they have seen
on TV.

2. *Limit the amount of TV.* If you say, "You may
watch two [or whatever number you choose] programs each evening," your child needs to read the
TV schedule to make critical judgments about which
two programs to watch. When children know that
you value reading, they begin to pick up your values.

3. *Know what TV programs your children watch.*
Mr. Rogers' Neighborhood, Reading Rainbow, and
Sesame Street have educational value that leads to
extended reading. TV shows like *Life Goes On* and
The Wonder Years cover important issues; talk with
your children about the issues and the shows they
enjoy most to develop taste and discrimination in
their viewing. Watch TV with them so they can discuss parts they don't understand or find frightening.

4. *Build bridges between TV shows and books.*
For example, if you see a news program about birds
caught in an oil spill, get books from the library on

endangered species, how to care for the environment, or cleaning up oil spills.

5. *Talk with your child about TV programs*. Children have questions about what they see on TV; you need to discuss their misconceptions and questions. Use TV episodes as a beginning point for a family discussion. Make connections between books and TV. Talk about what happened on *The Wonder Years*, *Full House*, or *Life Goes On*, and what happens in your family. It might be that the episode is just like or just the opposite of what happens in your family. Talking with children about what they see helps clarify the differences between real life and televised stories.

6. *Find a quiet place for you and your child to read*. Even if the television set is on you can tune it out when you're absorbed with a good book. Children like snug, cozy places. Use pillows to create one behind the sofa, near a bed, or under the stairs. Go to a quiet room, if possible, but even if you need to be in the same room with the TV set, you can create a place apart for reading.

Activities for Special Times

Life is not all work and no play. There are weekends, summer vacations, school breaks, birthdays, holidays, rainy days, and snowy days. These are times that books make a difference. They are also days that provide a little more free time. There are times that books fill in long hours when a child is sick or in the hospital. Books are the right medicine for happy times and sad ones.

1. *Buy a birthday book.* When children receive a book for their birthday, they recognize that books are special gifts. If possible, send a book to your school library to celebrate your child's birthday. Some schools have bookplates to inscribe the name of the child who is honored by the book gift.

2. *Make a rainy day book.* Staple a few sheets of paper together to create a book with your child as the illustrator. Write down the sounds of rain — ping, splash, patter. Draw pictures of rain equipment — boots, raincoats, umbrellas. Draw pictures of your neighborhood in the rain — buildings, people, animals. Go to the library to get *Rain Talk* by Mary Serfoza, in which a child listens to the "ping a ding, plip plip, and drum-a-tum" sounds of the rain. Get *Umbrella* by Taro Yashima, in which three-year-old Momo is eager for the rain to come so she can use her new red boots and umbrella. Seeing what others do to celebrate the rain gives your children models for their own books.

3. *Read on snowy days.* When it's snowing, it's a good time to snuggle down cozily with a book. Try Ezra Jack Keats's *Snowy Day* in which Peter plays in the snow all day long. Peter hits a snow-covered branch, and tries to save a snowball for another day by putting it in his pocket. Do some of the things Peter does in his story with your child — make snow angels, hit snow-covered branches, build a snowman. Write out a recipe for snow ice cream and let your child follow the directions.

4. *Read before vacations.* When you are getting ready for a vacation, get some books from the library or travel agency. Read about the place you are going. Don't limit your reading to travel brochures, how-

ever. There are excellent informational books about the national parks, historical sites, and resort areas. There are also fictional stories set in all parts of the country and world. Ask your children's librarian to point out books set in the area you will be visiting.

If the books are too difficult for your child to manage reading alone, vary the pattern by reading them aloud. Your child learns that reading is a source of information for all endeavors.

5. *Read during vacations.* If you travel, books are a vital part of your luggage. Take books along. Encourage your child to keep a journal or diary. Write a book together about places you see. If you stay at home, books are an even more important part of vacation time. Set a quiet reading time each day. Vacations are the time to tackle thick books that take a week or so to read.

6. *Make a holiday book.* For each holiday, make a book with your child showing your family traditions. Include a section on special food, house decorations, family rituals, and activities.

You are not only involving your child in reading and writing but you are passing along your family heritage.

7. *Do crossword puzzles with your child.* People who work crosswork puzzles become wordsmiths — they pay attention to words. Do crossword puzzles with your child, saying, for example, "What is a three-letter word for feline?" Children learn that words have more than one meaning, they learn definitions, and they pay attention to the length of words. All these skills learned in fun will serve them well as readers and writers.

Did You Know . . .

Kids who are read to do better in school.

Reading aloud to a child raises her self-esteem and reading ability.

Becoming a better reader helps a child do better in social studies and math.

Keeping a diary helps a child become a better writer and reader.

Reading the print on cereal boxes is good practice for a child.

Allowing your child to read in bed is a good habit to start.

Children will read on their own a book that has been read aloud to them.

Chapter 5:
Preschoolers

Life with Preschoolers

INFANTS

- *Like action nursery rhymes*
- *Fall asleep to nursery songs and lullabies*
- *Listen to Mother Goose verses as they are rocked*
- *Imitate actions of children in books*
- *Participate in sounds of animals in books*

- *Relate books to real life*
- *Like to see babies in books*
- *Pick favorite books from shelf*
- *Need the three R's: rhythm, repetition, and rhyme*

In the great green room
There was a telephone
And a red balloon
And a picture of —
The cow jumping over the moon

I know this book, *Goodnight Moon*, by heart. As I read it to my youngest grandchild, Trisha, I'm always grateful that I have yet another chance to read all the old favorites once again. Trisha has been bathed in books since she was born; her mother, father, brother, and sister all read to her regularly. So do Grandma and Grandpa when we visit. At sixteen months of age, Trisha shows that books are an important part of her life.

If you read a book to Trisha with animals in it, she says, "grr, bow-wow, moo"; she makes the sound the animal makes and points to the picture of the animal as she says it. She also imitates the actions of children in books; when they clap their hands, she claps hers. When they jump up and down, Trisha jumps up and down. If the child in a book takes a bath, Trisha jumps down from your lap, tries to pull off her shirt and socks as she runs toward the tub. She says, "Bubble, Bubble," because she wants to take a bath, too. She is imitating what happens in books by doing the same in her life.

Trisha loves to look at pictures of babies in books.

She never tires of patting the picture and saying "Baby, Baby!" seemingly fascinated with someone who looks like her. Trisha carries books around with her, clutching them to her chest the same way she carries her teddy bear. She says, "Book, book," and goes to the shelf to get one as a means of asking someone to read to her.

Sixteen-month-old Trisha sits for half an hour to 45 minutes while someone reads to her and talks with her about the pictures. Of course, she isn't exactly sitting still all the time. She pats the babies, claps her hands, makes animal sounds, and generally does whatever the character in the book does. Some people say we need to "catch 'em in the cradle" to make children readers, but with Trisha we catch her on the run.

Pop-up books are a disaster after a session with Trisha. She has a perfect record with pop-ups; she has demolished every single one she has ever gotten her hands on. She grabs the picture that flips up and hands it to her mother to show her the pretty picture. She is fascinated by the movement and, quicker than you can grab her hand, she has grabbed the page. So much for another pop-up book. We have glued, taped, and stapled pieces to try to rescue Trisha-ized books. We'll have to wait until she's older to bring out any more.

As a grandmother, I know why we must read to our children, but as a young mother I did not realize its importance. I had been a kindergarten teacher for a few years and knew the place of books in a classroom but I didn't understand the critical need to have books at home.

Our children loved stories; when my father came

to visit he told our children the same stories he had told me as a child. They begged for more just as I had done. Grandpa's stories were most often about hunting wild animals and as the children got bigger so did the size of the wild animals he hunted. He matched the length of each scary chase through the woods to fit the length of their attention span. Today we do more book reading than storytelling to Trisha; perhaps we depend too much on other people's stories instead of our own. Children need both.

TODDLERS

- *Like to read the same books over and over*
- *Look at board books*
- *Pick out their favorite book from a shelf*
- *Repeat Mother Goose verses by heart*
- *Explore the world by tasting, climbing, touching it*
- *Like short rhyming stories*
- *Like large, clear, realistic pictures*
- *Like to name objects in books and magazines*
- *Like bathtub books and toy books*

Lucy and Kevin Coneys, ages three and four, have been surrounded by books since birth. Their mother, Anne, cannot get them into bed without a story or two — frequently the same story read again and again. Anne says, "I've had to read *Harriet's Halloween Candy* every night for the past two years. Lucy won't go to bed without it." Lucy makes up names for special books. She calls *Star Rocker*, the "Rocky" book. She calls a train book "Diggety Doo."

Anne takes Lucy and Kevin to the library every week. They listen to the story hour, do finger plays and crafts, before picking out the books they will take home. They walk out with a stack of 20 to 30 books each week and always beg for just one more.

One day Anne realized that things had been too quiet for longer than she ordinarily expected quiet moments to be. She hadn't heard a peep for more than half an hour so she tiptoed to the children's room to check on what was going on. There were the two children curled up on the bed with Lucy reading to Kevin.

Anne heard Kevin complain, "You didn't say about the penguin." It seemed Lucy had skipped over a detail of the story.

Board books are a favorite with Lucy and Kevin. Anne likes them because she doesn't have to keep reminding them, "Be careful. Watch out for the pages." These books are actually sturdy cardboard! Lucy and Kevin read durable board books alone. You find them in their toy box, in their beds, and even, once in a while, on shelves.

Recently, Aunt Maura invited Lucy over to spend the night. When her mother said it was all right, Lucy ran to her room to pack her suitcase. When her mother checked the suitcase, she found seven books in it, nothing else. She said to Lucy, "Where are your clothes?" Lucy replied, "Oh, I forgot." It is clear that

Lucy values books over anything else when she is going away from home.

PRESCHOOLERS

- *Use words to express themselves*
- *Struggle for independence: "wanna do it myself"*
- *Play with language, singsong, nonsense sounds*
- *Enjoy* Sesame Street *and Big Bird*
- *Are fascinated by other children, share grudgingly*
- *May create an imaginary friend*
- *Are fearful of the dark and strangers*
- *Like simple folktales but not fairy tales*

Luis Eduardo Dorado is a four year old, chock-full of energy. He charges in the door from nursery school ready to eat, play, watch TV, and annoy his mother all at the same time. His older sister, Marta, is a calming influence on him, but Marta is most often at school or out with her friends.

Luis must find ways to entertain himself alone. He throws every ounce of his 40 pounds, soaking wet, into his activities. He laughs outrageously one moment and bursts into tears the next. His twinkling black eyes sparkle with devilment, humor, or displeasure depending upon his mood of the moment.

Today Marta is teaching Luis a new song, "The Eensy Weensy Spider." She sings it a couple of times using the hand motions and Luis joins her on the second round. He overdoes the motions crashing his hands down on Marta's head as he shouts, "Down comes the rain." Marta frowns and threatens to end the game if he continues acting up. The threat of losing the attention of his big sister that he adores works! Marta picks up the refrain and tries to get Luis to point the forefingers and stick up the thumbs on both hands to imitate the spider's movements climbing up the waterspout. This action is a bit too complicated for Luis's four-year-old coordination; he wiggles all his fingers as he mimics the spider crawling up the waterspout.

Marta decides to give Luis another way to interpret the spider and the waterspout song. She gives him a marker and a big piece of paper. Luis happily scribbles on the paper, making large circular movements as he sings about the spider crawling up the waterspout. He brings his marker down hard across the page with a whoosh when the rain comes down, and starts all over again spiraling the spider marks back up the page. The finished product looks mostly like big round scribbles but Marta decides that it's good enough to tape on the refrigerator door. Marta says, "Now that we are here at the refrigerator, maybe it's time for a little juice and crackers." After Luis settles down, Marta pulls out a pop-up book about the eensy weensy spider. Luis handles it tenderly because it is a special gift from a special person in his life. He reads it like an angel, gently pulling out the tabs to make the spider move.

Making a Reader Out of
Your Preschooler

You have all the preschool years to send an important message to your child: Reading is fun! There is *no* direct teaching, such as "What is that word or letter?" That comes later. Right now, it's all pleasure. Of course, you will talk about the story and the characters.

You may ask, "What do you think is going to happen next?" You'll answer questions, too — any that your child asks. But you don't ask questions the way a teacher asks questions. You sort of ponder out loud, "Mmmm, wonder what he's going to do now?" Your questions don't require an answer, you're just keeping the interest focused on the story.

When you pick up a new book, you might say, "I wonder what this story is going to be about?" This question introduces and underscores a very important message — that a story *is about* something. You are indicating that a story has meaning and that we discover the meaning by reading the words. That's the real reason for reading. You are laying the basic groundwork for a lasting understanding. Reading is getting meaning. You may wonder why I'm making such an issue of this simple concept. It's because I've seen children say the words perfectly on a page and yet when I ask them, "What did you just read?" they say, "I don't know."

This is the difference between simply pronouncing the sounds and real reading (getting meaning). Children who settle for just pronouncing sounds become the students who have problems reading in school — they don't expect reading to make sense! Good readers expect things to make sense; they settle for nothing less.

This is not to say that we don't read nonsense verse, jingles, and made-up words. When we read Dr. Seuss's *On Beyond Zebra*, we giggle at the make-believe words and animals. When we say jingly Mother Goose rhymes, we laugh at the word play and say the delicious sounds over again. Children take their cues from the way you behave; you are their model.

When you are reading to your preschooler, invite her to join in on the repetitive phrases — she'll do it automatically anyway. If the print for some word is larger, read it louder; if it's wiggly or wavy, read it in a wavering voice; if it's tiny, read it softly; you're showing her that we get clues from print. Saying words from print along with you is a beginning step, just the way she held onto your finger as she took those first wobbly steps in walking.

Preschoolers like to fill in the gaps when you read together. Start this with Mother Goose or other rhyming words and continue the practice with non-rhyming texts. Read "Humpty Dumpty sat on a ——. Humpty Dumpty had a great ——." Children know which word to insert because it rhymes or makes sense. This builds an expectation that they know what words will come next.

Everything you do when you read to your preschooler is paving the way for him to read alone. When a kindergarten teacher opens a book to read to five year olds, *your* child will know what to expect and how to participate. Children learn how to hold a book, how to turn pages, and how to enjoy a story from hearing stories at home. You are making a reader out of your child.

Making a Writer Out of Your Preschooler

The connections between early reading and early writing are still being explored, but we already know some things for sure. We know that there are certain developmental stages all children seem to go through. Children gradually discover aspects of writing that we take for granted, such as capital letters, periods, and words going across a page. Seemingly, children discover them in a somewhat similar order. Children gradually discover that writing (at least in English) goes from left to right. They learn that we keep the letters on a straight line going across a page. They learn that words are represented by letters, that words are separated by a space, and that meaning comes from the words and not the pictures. For a long time, children do not distinguish between writing and drawing. One day in a kindergarten class, I asked Billy what he was going to write about. He said, "How do I know? I haven't even drawed it yet."

Children seem to draw first and write later. We help them if we write down what they say about their pictures. Similarly, we know that children write first and read later; one helps the other. Writing calls attention to print and shows that letters represent sounds; that knowledge opens the door to reading.

Children move from primitive drawing skill to the ability to form the letter "O" or to make circles. Individual experiences differ greatly, but there are general writing patterns you might watch for. Their early attempts will be gross approximations and from there they move to finer distinctions. It's the same way in speaking. Children first call all men "Daddy" but then narrow that term down to the one person who is their father. They call all four-legged animals "horseys" until they refine the categories and call some doggies, cows, or zebras.

Writing development depends a lot upon eye-hand motor coordination, as well as visual perception. Children can distinguish between letter forms before they are able to actually write them. In this, as in all learning, let the child be the guide. Don't insist that he make the letters the way you do; he'll come to that gradually. When you think about the letters of the alphabet as 50-plus geometric forms, you realize how much your child has to remember. The uppercase letters don't look a whole lot like lowercase letters — and yet we call them the same thing. Adults learning the Greek alphabet are just as perplexed as children learning English, and yet we know the alphabetic principle that words are represented by letters that proceed across a page and are separated by spaces. A child will insist that "Cindy" is not her name; her name is "CINDY."

The first word your child will write is probably her own name. Stick with uppercase (capital) letters so that she sees it the same way for a while. Kindergarten teachers are happy that children know how to write their names; they will later teach them the finer distinctions of upper and lowercase letters.

Tips for Busy Parents

During the preschool years, your child is a learning machine — he learns even when you don't know he's learning. The most important things you want your child to do are:

- *To get to know about books*
- *To come to love books*
- *To learn about language*

You can accomplish these worthy learning tasks if you do some simple things.

1. *Read a bedtime story.* This ritual cannot be established too early or repeated too often. These enjoyable times when you and your child are close together are essential in establishing a lifelong habit.

2. *Read the same books over and over.* You may get bored like the father who said, "If I have to read *Goodnight Moon* one more time, I think I'll die." For your child it is the repetition of a happy experience, one she wants again and again.

3. *Give your child markers or paper and pencils.* Children need to make marks on paper to learn that what we say can be written down and that they can write, too. I know you don't like marks on your walls or furniture any more than I do but don't deny your child this crucial learning experience. Supervise your preschooler's writing. Keep writing supplies in a special place that you bring out while you are peeling potatoes and can keep an eye on the writer.

4. *Give your child a blackboard and chalk.* Small hand-held or easel-type blackboards are inexpensive; sometimes they are discarded by a school. Set up the blackboard in the kitchen where you can talk to your child while she is writing.

5. *Write messages to your child.* When you need to be away, leave a message to be read to your child.

Isaac Lubow's mother works but she puts a little poem or message in his lunch box every day.

6. *Label your child's possessions.* Name tags are not to be used just when packing for camp. If clothes are to be handed down to the next child — as we all do — use just the last name or initials. Children need to see their names on everything.

7. *Get alphabet books and make alphabet books.* See your local libraries for some good alphabet books. Make your own alphabet book. Staple together 26 pages of paper, write a letter on each page. Your child fills each page with words or pictures that begin with that letter. She can cut the pictures from old magazines or draw them herself. She can write her name and the names of her friends on the appropriate pages. You can help when necessary.

8. *Put magnetic letters on the refrigerator.* Many children have learned to read from magnetic letters on the refrigerator. Of course, you need to form them into words, especially your child's name, and invite him to do the same. We put things on the refrigerator that we want people to notice. My friend Norman Teitel wrote a story for his granddaughter. When he called to see if she had received and enjoyed it, he asked, "What did you do with it?" She answered primly, "I put it on the refrigerator."

Surefire Hits for Preschoolers

Janet and Allan Ahlberg. *Each Peach Pear Plum.* Viking, 1979.

A perfect book for preschoolers. Play the I Spy game with familiar nursery rhyme characters. Say part of the verse and let your child finish the rhyme.

Molly Bang. *Ten, Nine, Eight.* Greenwillow, 1983.
A father and daughter count backwards to get one little girl all ready for bed.

Donald Crews. *Freight Train.* Greenwillow, 1978.
Watch an empty railroad track fill up with a red caboose, an orange tank car, a yellow hopper car, green cattle car, blue gondola, purple boxcar, and a black steam engine, before it becomes a ribbon of color zooming through tunnels.

Kate Greenaway. *A Apple Pie.* Warne, 1886.
Sing through the alphabet with all the things that happened to the apple pie.

Sarah Josepha Hale. *Mary Had a Little Lamb.* Photo-illustrated by Bruce McMillan. Scholastic, 1990.
The well-known poem is illustrated here in a colorful, eye-opening way with gorgeous color photos.

Tana Hoban. *Count and See.* Macmillan, 1972.
Clear photographs of familiar objects to count and count again up to fifteen.

Pat Hutchins. *Rosie's Walk.* Macmillan, 1968.
Rosie merely takes a walk around the barnyard but she evades a fox every step of the way. The fox gets trapped and children see the words *over, under, across, around,* and *through* illustrated.

Ezra Jack Keats. *The Snowy Day.* Viking, 1962.
Peter goes out to play in the snow and tries to save

a snowball by putting it in his pocket.

Ruth Krauss. *The Carrot Seed.* Illustrated by Crockett Johnson. Harper, 1945.
A determined little boy plants a carrot seed and, despite warnings that it won't come up, waits patiently for his big carrot to grow. Grow, it does.

Arnold Lobel. *On Market Street.* Illustrated by Anita Lobel. Greenwillow, 1981.
In an intriguing alphabet book, go shopping with a child who meets people shaped from the products they sell.

H. A. Rey. *Curious George.* Houghton Mifflin, 1941.
A little monkey, George, lets his curiosity get him into a lot of trouble, but the man with the yellow hat helps him out.

Nancy Tafuri. *Have You Seen My Duckling?* Greenwillow, 1984.
Mother Duck takes her brood out to swim but one little duckling goes off to explore the world alone. Preschoolers happily find the missing duckling each time the mother asks, "Have you seen my duckling?"

Did You Know . . .

Young children like to hear the same story over and over again. They need to hear the same story repeatedly to make it their own.
Children like to participate in story reading and storytelling. Look for books with flaps to lift or

parts that fold out. Let your child turn the pages. Let your child say the words he knows.

Children need to see that reading and writing are useful and enjoyable things to do before they begin to work on remembering letter names.

Reading stories and poems to children is the best way to teach them to read.

Children's natural curiosity and desire to make sense of their world are the only motivation they need to learn.

Children learn by doing things — actively exploring books and print.

Chapter 6:
Five and
Six Year Olds

Life with Five and Six Year Olds

FIVE YEAR OLDS

- *Like stories with animals that talk*
- *Like simple folktales and some fairy tales*
- *Like a prince and a princess*
- *Believe in magic*
- *Think fairy tale characters lived a long time ago*
- *Sometimes confuse real and make-believe*

- *Recognize some letters of the alphabet*
- *Can write their name*

Five- and six-year-old children are voracious language learners. They seem to absorb new words from the very air they breathe. When children are given opportunities to *use* the language they learn, they show amazing progress. Michael Romero, described below, is unique but not unusual in his ability to use language vividly.

Five-year-old Michael and his little brother are the light of their father's life. His dad has been tossing a softball to Mike since he was old enough to stand, so naturally Mike likes sports and wants to be a baseball player when he grows up. When his dad comes home from his factory job, he has a tickle fight with Mike. You can't tell who wins but the tussle and screams of mock pain rouse the neighbors. His father is a big tease but he is devoted to giving Michael every educational advantage that he himself never had. His father bought him a computer when he was in kindergarten; Michael learned his ABCs on the computer and used the computer at school to learn to write using invented spelling. Mike became so familiar with the computer that he could write his stories on it. Here is one story Michael wrote:

> My bruthr had the chicin pox.
> dad told him that hee is
> gowing to get a beec and litl wit
> fethrs growing awt of his armpits.
> and a litl red com wil grow awt of
> the top of his hed. hee got scard.

I didnt get scard beecorz I noow hee
wuz onleey teesing.

Mike received so much praise for his writing ability
that he wrote even more. He likes to have poetry read
to him for the bedtime story and most often it is his
father who does the reading. Like many children Michael draws upon the words he hears for the words
he writes. Here is another sample of his work:

This is a storey about me,
Wen I snees the holl worlld spins a
rouwnd wen I snees the flours blow
awa and wen I snees the gras jumps.
And wen I snees the holl room shacs.
And wen I snees evereey botey ses
Michael you are to louwd.

Michael's father has devoted endless time, effort,
and love to his son. There is little doubt that the
investment is paying off in big dividends.

Five-year-old Emily and her three-year-old-brother
Andrew hear about six stories a day; both Mom and
Dad read to them. The children connect the stories
they hear to real life. When birds came up to the
feeder last winter, Andrew went to find *A Year of
Birds* by Ashley Wolff and pointed to the feeding sta-
tion. When Andrew lost his teddy bear, Emily said
he was just like the boy in *The Blanket,* John Burn-
ingham's book; he had everybody in the house looking for it. Everyone looked for Andrew's bear the same
way everybody had looked for the lost blanket; both
were found under their owner's pillow. Emily has her
favorite stories: she has memorized *Brown Bear,*

Brown Bear; and she loves to recite everything *The Very Hungry Caterpillar* ate on Saturday. She quietly hands *Cookie's Week* to a guest for a third reading and whispers confidentially, "Andrew can't read yet!" Emily can't read yet either but luckily she doesn't know it.

Emily was an emergent reader, memorizing books, joining in on refrains, retelling stories to Andrew, and connecting them to her own life. Six months later, Emily was a reader. She had played at reading until she became a real reader.

SIX YEAR OLDS

- *Recognize the letters of the alphabet*
- *Can count to 100*
- *Can write about 10 words from memory*
- *Are able to read easy-to-read books*
- *Still like fairy tales*
- *Like being read to*
- *Memorize poetry and nonsense verse*
- *Enjoy alphabet and counting books*
- *Search for simple informational books*
- *Like books about dinosaurs*
- *Write with invented spellings*

As I located seat 6C on the plane, I smiled to find

a child and her mother as my seatmates. In a few minutes I discovered that the winsome child was named Lauren, that she was six years old, in the first grade, and that she was on her way to serve as flower girl in her auntie's wedding. Before long, I pulled two books by Bill Martin, Jr., *Brown Bear, Brown Bear* and *Chicka Chicka Boom Boom*, out of my book bag and read them with Lauren.

I read the first page, "Brown Bear, Brown Bear, what do you see? I see a Red Bird looking at me."

Lauren picked up the patterned language quickly and read the next page, "Red Bird, Red Bird, what do you see? I see a Yellow Duck looking at me." She also grasped the pattern of the other book, "A told B, and B told C, I'll meet you at the top of the coconut tree. Chicka chicka boom boom! Will there be enough room?"

Together we enjoyed the lilting rhythmic flow of Bill Martin's words as we sailed through the sky toward Minneapolis. It was easy for Lauren to chime in readily to read along with me, because she identified the strong pattern and knew what was coming next; she could predict the words because they rhymed and sounded like real language. Like all beginning readers, Lauren read more fluently because the books had natural-sounding, rhythmic language.

I told Lauren's mother how impressed I was with Lauren's ability to read. Lauren was a beginning first-grader and yet she could read along with the rhythmic pattern of the language in the stories easily. Later during the flight Lauren showed me the reading book she carried with her from school. It was stuffed with several worksheets assigned for Lauren to complete "so she wouldn't miss anything" while she was away on flower-girl duty. Lauren's book contained the following story:

> Ann ran. Nan ran.
> Ann and Nan ran and ran.
> Ann ran to Nan.
> Nan ran to Ann.

Lauren read this, too, but she read it more slowly and haltingly than she read the other stories. The short stilted sentences made word by word reading a necessity. The language in her school book does not sound like phrases we would say in real life. There is nothing inherently interesting in the school book story, but there is in the Bill Martin books. Maybe that's why Lauren reads them so easily. The worksheets, filled with pictures to match to words, spaces to write a word, and outlines to color in, contained the same stilted vocabulary. This bright, competent child was working far below her ability level and the language in her reading book was doing little to enrich her vocabulary.

Making a Reader Out of Your Five and Six Year Old

Five and six year olds have a growing attention span; they are willing to stick with some tasks for nearly an hour, depending on how much interest they have. This means we can read longer and more complex stories to them. Fives and sixes are on the verge of figuring out how to read for themselves; they ask endless questions, such as "What does that say?"

Some children have already figured out how letters combine to make words and are striking out on their own as early readers. They need different material — short, simple, and rhythmic language. Even precocious readers' eyes tire easily at this age: try to keep reading sessions brief, happy, and successful.

Five and six year olds are developing a growing sense of independence, going off to school alone, dressing themselves, and caring for their personal needs. These signs bode well for intellectual development since the child can seek out information that interests her. Independence at this age, however, is like thin ice on a pond; it collapses easily if tested too strongly. Home and family provide the security that makes five and six year olds brave and strong within their small circle of success.

Many five- and six-year-old children are fearful: scared of the dark, strangers, and monsters. Their understanding of the line between real and make-believe is not firmly fixed; they don't like to take chances in case some of those monsters in books are real! They may want a certain book put away or taken out of their room before they can fall asleep.

For example, Maurice Sendak's book, *Where the Wild Things Are*, has huge smiling monster wild things who are completely under Max's control. The wild things don't want Max to leave their land but he chooses to be where someone loves him best of all — home. When a child enjoys this book wrapped in the security of a parent's arms, there is nothing to fear. If your child feels differently about it, just put the book away for a while — he will laugh at it later.

Making a Writer Out of Your Five and Six Year Old

Five and six year olds love to make marks on paper; they are far beyond the scribble stage and are making real letters and words. They use both pictures and letters, mixing them freely to put their meanings on paper. During this period children are working on the relationships between letters and sounds. They try to figure these out by themselves, and many children succeed.

As children become writers, they invent spellings for words they want to use. Invented spelling is what we call children's misspellings before they learn all the rules adults use to spell. Children's errors give us a window on what they know. If a child spells dinosaur "dnsr" we see that he is using beginning sounds heavily and is relying on the consonant sounds instead of vowels. This is exactly what he should be doing at his developmental stage.

Invented spelling does *not* interfere with children's ability to spell correctly later. It is an appropriate developmental step just like the "mmmm" and "dddd" sounds your child made as a beginning speaker. There are lots of advantages for the child who uses invented spelling, however. Here are some:

INVENTED SPELLING

- *Encourages children to figure out the alphabet*
- *Makes children independent as writers; they don't have to ask others how to spell*

words; it frees them from depending on others

- *Encourages children to write longer, more colorful stories; they can write anything they can say; writing more = writing better*
- *Moves children beyond words they know how to read; they are not limited to writing only words they can read; it helps them learn to read*
- *Encourages children to take responsibility for their own learning; they are in control of what they write and how they write it; they make the writing system their own*
- *Provides extensive practice in phonics; children practice their sounds as they write — using letters to represent the sounds they hear in words*

Inventive spellers use the names of the letters and not just the sounds we say the letters represent. For example, they begin *elephant* with "L," spell *you* "U," and *why* "Y." They learn to use long vowels (ā as in cake) before short vowels (ă as in task) because they hear the sound of the letter name in the long vowels. Developmental stages in invented spelling hinge upon technical and complicated detail; you only need to encourage your child to use invented spelling and watch it grow toward standard spelling.

Here is a sample from a five year old:

I WAT TO GRAT EDAVAHER
I WAT ON A
FARES WEL AD A ROLRKSDA.
John, age 5, P.S. 230, Brooklyn
(Translation: I went to Great Adventure [a local amusement park]. I went on a Ferris wheel and a roller coaster.)

Another five year old, in California, wrote this:

I love riten becaes I wat to lrn to red. (Translation: I love writing because I want to learn to read.)

Parents are concerned that their children will eventually learn how to spell correctly. Let me assure you that invented spelling is a developmental step; children go on to learn to spell even better than they would if they had not been allowed to take these beginning steps. Most importantly, they become much better writers earlier because they are encouraged to use invented spellings. Children write more and learn to read more easily because of the confidence it gives them to master print.

Tips for Busy Parents

Joanne Sebetic, a reading teacher at Guggenheim School, in Port Washington, New York, has a son, Steve, who had difficulty learning to read in the first grade. Figuring out each word was so slow and painful that Steve never seemed to get any fun from reading. He couldn't concentrate on the meaning because he was struggling so hard to figure out the words. Joanne talked with Steve's teacher and they made a plan. Each day, Steve brought home a book from school and Joanne would read one page and Steve would read the next. They would cuddle up in a chair or Joanne would lie beside him on his bed and they would take turns reading. A few months later, Steve's teacher called Joanne and said, "Whatever you're doing is really working. Steve is just zooming along with reading. He has caught fire as a reader and is making terrific progress." The assisted reading that Joanne did with Steve seemed to be the key to fluent reading for him.

1. *You read to me and I'll read to you.* Beginning readers need help in moving from word-to-word reading to smooth meaningful reading. Take turns reading with your child. You read one page and let the child read the next.

2. *Fill in the blanks.* Reading poetry and verse that rhymes is a terrific way to lead your five or six year old into reading. Read the phrases all the way through for part of the poem or verse. Then stop before you reach the end of the next rhyming line and let your child provide the rhyming word.

3. *Play sounds games.* While you are preparing a meal, driving, or cleaning, play a game about sounds with your child. A simple starter is: "Riddle, riddle, ree. I see something you don't see. And it starts with T." Your child guesses what you see and takes the next turn. Start with the sounds at the beginnings of words, they are the ones children pay most atten-

tion to. As your child becomes more sophisticated, you can move to the sounds at the ends of words. ". . . and it ends with K."

4. *Make a calendar.* Use one sheet of paper for each month. Write the days of the week across the top and put in the numeral 1 for the first day of the month. Let your child finish the calendar writing in special events coming up. Whether you do one month or an entire year depends on your child's maturity and your patience.

5. *Write a fill-in-the-blank story.* Make up a simple story frame or use a familiar folktale, such as "The Three Little Pigs." Write "Once upon a time there were _____ . They told their _____ they were going out to seek their _____." Your child fills in the names of the characters and other important words. Invented spelling should be praised.

6. *Write a biography or autobiography.* Five- and six-year-old children like to write about themselves. With your help, they can write their autobiography. Use the same technique of writing in parts that are too difficult and allowing your child to fill in names and important words. For example, "_____ was born on _____ . S/he weighed _____ pounds and _____ ounces. The first visitor was _____."

7. *Make a jigsaw puzzle.* Use a poster, a picture postcard, the dust jacket from a book, or a large color picture from a magazine. Paste the picture or laminate it to a shirt cardboard. Cut the stiff pieces into odd shapes to make a jigsaw puzzle.

8. *Make a board game.* Choose one of your child's favorite books as the basis for a board game. Use the

events or episodes in the book to divide steps along a path the characters must travel. Use small objects to represent the characters. Make a spinner to determine how many steps each player can take. The object of the game is to see who arrives first at the end of the story.

9. *Start a memory box.* Create dividers in a small box to hold objects your child collects. A walk in the woods will lead to acorns, nuts, leaves, small stones, bird feathers, and seed pods. A walk in your neighborhood may lead to pebbles, keys, coins, and who knows what. A walk along the beach will lead to seashells and driftwood. A collection of objects related to a favorite book is even more fun. Label the objects in the collection to involve reading and writing.

10. *Cooking from a book.* Prepare some food inspired by a book. For example, *Chicken Soup with Rice*, *Green Eggs and Ham* and *Watch Out for Chicken Feet in Your Soup* are naturals. Many books include recipes for the character's favorite food. Look for cookbooks based on Laura Ingalls Wilder, Mary Poppins, and A. A. Milne books.

Surefire Hits for Five and Six Year Olds

Marcia Brown. *The Three Billy Goats Gruff.* Harcourt, 1957.

A vibrant retelling of three clever goats who outsmart the mean old troll.

Virginia Lee Burton. *Mike Mulligan and His Steam Shovel.* Houghton Mifflin, 1939.

Mike Mulligan finds a perfect place to use his steam shovel, Mary Anne, when she is replaced by newer machines.

Wanda Ga'g. *Millions of Cats.* Coward McCann, 1928.
A little old man searches for the prettiest cat in the world to give to his wife. He sees hundreds of cats, thousands of cats, millions and billions and trillions of cats. Children join in on the refrain.

Russell Hoban. *A Baby Sister for Frances.* Illustrated by Lillian Hoban. Harper, 1964.
Frances, an adorable badger, finds it hard to accept the newcomer in her family until she learns how important a big sister can be. See also: *Bedtime for Frances, Bread and Jam for Frances, Best Friends for Frances,* and *A Bargain for Frances.*

Arnold Lobel. *Frog and Toad Are Friends.* Harper, 1970.
Short easy-to-read stories about two loyal friends. The warmth and humor appeal to child and adult alike.

Jan Slepian and Ann Seidler. *The Hungry Thing.* Illustrated by Richard E. Martin. Scholastic, 1988.
A hungry creature comes to town and asks for things to eat; he asks for what he wants by asking for it in rhyme. Children quickly figure it out. See also: *The Hungry Thing Returns.*

Maurice Sendak. *Where the Wild Things Are.* Harper, 1963.

Max's mother sends him off to bed without his supper, but he goes to the land where the wild things are. The monsters there love him and feel sad when he returns to where someone loves him best of all — home.

Esphyr Slobodkina. *Caps for Sale.* HarperCollins, 1947.
A peddlar comes to sell caps, red caps, yellow caps, all for fifty cents a cap. When he takes a nap under a tree, monkeys steal his caps; he has a difficult time getting them back.

Bernard Waber. *Ira Sleeps Over.* Houghton Mifflin, 1972.
Ira wonders if he should take his teddy bear when he's invited to sleep over at Reggie's house. Wonderful family interplay.

Taro Yashima. *Crow Boy.* Viking, 1955.
Crow Boy receives his nickname from the imitations he does of voices of crows from his distant village. Acceptance is hard won for a child who is considered different.

Did You Know . . .

Children who know how to handle books and are familiar with stories learn how to read much faster than those who have little or no book experience. Children who learn to read early are the ones who are read to by parents, siblings, or other caregivers.

Reading aloud to your child is the single most important thing you can do to make him a reader.

Telling a story from the pictures is an important step in the learning-to-read process.

Pretend reading is a critical step in the developmental process of learning to read.

Talking develops language. Talk to your child and get her to talk about things you do together and things she does with friends.

Chapter 7:
Seven and Eight
Year Olds

Life with Seven and Eight Year Olds

SEVEN YEAR OLDS

- *Develop budding friendships*
- *Seek acceptance by other children their age*
- *Show increasing independence from home and family*
- *Strike out on their own as readers*
- *Take pride in showing off their reading skill*
- *Understand more complex stories than they can read*

- *See the world as good/bad; fair/not fair*
- *Believe in magic*
- *Accept fairy tale "eye for an eye" morality and cruel justice*

Jamal, age seven, likes to go to the park by herself but her mother insists she can only go when her ten-year-old sister, Kyla, can be there, too. Jamal thinks Kyla is bossy; she tries to get away from her at the park because Jamal has her own friends and feels she's big enough to take care of herself. Today, though, she had seen Kyla talking to a boy and could hardly wait to get home to tell her mother. She knew her mother would say, "Good for you, Jamal. Kyla knows she's not supposed to be talking to boys at the park." Usually it was Kyla reporting what Jamal had done wrong — going down the slide headfirst and landing on her face in the sawdust, or standing up on the swings, the big swings reserved for bigger kids. Jamal felt important and was eager to see that justice was done — what's fair is fair! She hoped Kyla would get a spanking or be sent to her room. Then she and her mother would be alone; she would have her mother all to herself.

As they barged in the door of their apartment, Jamal began her report of Kyla's misbehavior, but her mother seemed to be amused instead of angry. How could that be? Mother always took Kyla seriously when she told about Jamal's misdeeds. Jamal was even more upset when Kyla told her version, "Momma, I was just talking to Steve because we have to do a report at school. He's almost finished with his part and I haven't even started. Besides, Jamal came over and started yelling at me right in front of Steve. I was embarrassed and so was Steve." Jamal could hardly believe her ears — how could Kyla be so unfair! She was only doing what was right!

Jamal decided that life certainly was not fair when Mother decided both girls needed to spend a little time alone. "Jamal, go to your room and Kyla, you sit right down here at this kitchen table and get to work on that school report." A big pout spread across Jamal's face. She jabbed her hands on her hips and stomped into the room she shared with Kyla. She pretended to be busy and ignored Kyla when she came in to get her schoolbag. Jamal flopped on her bed and hugged her teddy bear who always understood that she was brave and kind and good — not a tattletale or somebody to be ashamed of like Kyla said.

Gradually tears stopped leaking out of her eyes and the feelings of righteous indignation eased away. She felt cozy and self-important lying there looking at all of *her* things: the Barbie dolls, the pictures of her friends from school, and her books. She knew somebody who would understand — Ramona! She took comfort in reading Beverly Cleary's book about Ramona the Brave, who herself was often misunderstood. Slowly she opened her book and soon was lost in sharing another life with a girl her age who had troubles of her own. Someday people will appreciate me, she thought.

As a young mother, I sometimes read aloud a few picture books left over from my teaching days, but I didn't make a point of taking my children to the library or building their home book collection. This began to change as firstborn Janie entered second grade. She wanted books she could try to read alone, so we went to the public library to see if we could find any. Janie, like many other children, led her parents into children's books.

When I finally took Janie to the library we chanced upon Elsa Minarik's Little Bear books that were illustrated by Maurice Sendak. Little did I realize that Janie was selecting books by one of the world's foremost illustrators. By looking at the world through a child's eyes, Janie and I discovered Ezra Jack Keats's *The Snowy Day*, Maurice Sendak's *Where the Wild Things Are*, and Marcia Brown's *Cinderella*. Janie continued to take me with her into exploring books of increasing complexity as she grew as a reader. While she was developing her wings as an independent reader, Janie discovered chapter books on the C shelf at the library; she read like a rabbit nibbling carrots, through the books of Beverly Cleary, Eleanor Clymer, Matt Christopher, Scott Corbett, Natalie Savage Carlson, Rebecca Caudill, Molly Cone, and Elizabeth Coatsworth.

One day, friend and mentor Charlotte Huck gave me a copy of *Charlotte's Web* inscribed to "Bee and her family." I read this book aloud to the entire family. We laughed. We cried. We snuffled our way through at many points when I became choked up while reading about the friendship between a pig and a spider. This was the first truly significant children's novel I had ever read or my children had heard. It was a peak experience in our family. We began to look for more like it. We discovered A. A. Milne in *When We Were Very Young, Now We Are Six, Winnie-*

the-Pooh, and *The House at Pooh Corner*. We discovered Beatrix Potter's *The Tale of Peter Rabbit* and all her other animal books. We suppressed giggles and tears again through Kenneth Grahame's *The Wind in the Willows*. I remember sitting beside the children's bathtub to read the chapter "The Piper at the Gates of Dawn" and watched small tears slide down already wet faces. We puzzled our way through Lewis Carroll's *Alice in Wonderland*.

Of course we read other books, too, but these memorable ones became part of our lives. Even today we say, "He's a real Templeton" about a person who only does things for his own benefit, "Yes, Piglet" to a copycat, or "He's a Toad" about a show-off. So many things happened during those years that were to last a lifetime. We forged bonds of love, we all became readers, and I, unknowingly, laid the foundation for my own career devoted to children's books.

EIGHT YEAR OLDS

- *Reach peak of interest in fairy tales*
- *Begin interest in stories of real life*
- *Show beginning interest in sports*
- *Choose to read independently*
- *Like poetry/verse and chapter books*
- *Like riddles, jokes, off-the-wall humor*

- *Want to choose their own books*
- *Think picture books are babyish*

I spent a week baby-sitting with our three grand-children so their parents could take a much needed vacation. That week eight-year-old Jason and I cleaned out his bookshelves. It was easy to pull out books Jason had outgrown. We just put them on another shelf to keep until his little sister, Trisha, would grow into them. It was harder to sift out the superficial books he had collected. I wondered if he would ever read the comic books again or if they were just a passing interest? Jason is a child who doesn't like to throw anything away, so we agreed to put all potential discards into a box and allow him a last chance to rescue any treasures before the box went to the garage sale.

While we worked, I could tell which books Jason loved and which ones he was lukewarm about. When I picked up a Beverly Cleary book about Ramona, Jason grabbed it out of my hand and said, "That goes right here!" He tucked those books neatly on his shelf. He did the same with Matt Christopher sports books, Donald Sobol's Encyclopedia Brown books, and his current fad — Mad Libs. He also grabbed the Shel Silverstein books, *Where the Side-walk Ends* and *The Light in the Attic*. In fact, he put Shel Silverstein's books on his bedside table because he reads himself to sleep with the giggle-producing verses. When we'd finished, Jason's bookshelves re-flected his interests, his age, and his reading ability.

Jason's mom and stepfather both work; it's hard

to make ends meet with three kids. They don't have money to waste so when they buy a book they want to make sure it's one Jason will like for a long time and read over and over. No family can own all the books a child should read so Jason's family, like other families, turn to the library because it is free. Jason borrows books from both the public library and his school library. When he buys a book, it's most often a paperback from a series he knows he likes.

Like most eight-year-olds, Jason has nonstop energy. He more often runs than walks. He bounces on a bed instead of getting into it. He moves across a room like a streak of lightning and leaves a trail of pillows or papers in his tracks. He's interested in everything from guppies and snakes to outer space. He plays softball, soccer, badminton, or anything you can throw, hit, kick, or catch. But he likes to read and to be read to. The only sure way I could get him to sit still was to read to him. When I read to him he turns into an avid listener.

Jason is a reader for the simple reason that he has been read to. His mother reads to him at night to quiet him down from high-speed activity to sleepy time. His stepfather reads with him from nature magazines, fishing books, and hunting guides because he is an outdoorsman. His grandpa reads Irish folktales and riddle and joke books to him. And I read to him as a special part of every visit.

On Christmas Eve, I always read *The Polar Express* and *The Night Before Christmas* to keep curious little people busy while Santa and his helpers arrange gifts and surprises under the tree. Jason is also a reader because he reads by himself and has discovered that reading is fun. When he reads to his little sister, he props Trisha in his lap and reads Mother Goose verses to her. Since his patience is the same length as a firecracker, he cuts the session short if Trisha grabs for the page or squirms about too much. Jason is beginning to pass on the torch, a love of reading, that has been handed down to him.

During the week of baby-sitting, I chose *My Brother Sam Is Dead* as the book to read aloud. It was a book that would keep eleven-year-old Kali interested and yet not be too complex for Jason to understand. We read every night at bedtime but we still had about three chapters to finish when it was time for me to go to the airport. Along with my suitcase, Jason carried the book to the car. While their mother drove to the airport, I read aloud. While we waited at the terminal until it was time for me to board my plane, I read aloud. I felt frazzled as I ran down the ramp, the last one to get on the plane. I smiled when their mother called to say she had to finish reading the few remaining pages to Kali and Jason at the airport before they started home. That convinced me that Janie is taking her place in handing down the magic. It also convinced me that my grandchildren are growing up as readers who are hooked by a good story. I was also thankful that I was the grandmother and didn't need to cope with all that energy twenty-four hours a day, seven days a week, twelve months a year! I was exhausted!

Making a Reader Out of Your Seven and Eight Year Old

To help your child become a reader, look for books

that make sense — books that deal with things that are important in the real world. Jason and his friend like things that crawl and things that fly. Once they found three garter snakes in the park and put them in a pail. When they showed them off to neighbors who came to their garage sale they were promptly sent to the backyard. On the next trip to the library, the librarian helped them find Patricia Lauber's book, *Snakes Are Hunters*. They insisted on having some sections read to them immediately while they continued to look at the photographs to identify the snakes in their collection.

Seven and eight year olds also catch dragonflies, capture praying mantises, and fill jars with fireflies. Finding Julie Brinckloe's *Fireflies*, Bianca Lavies's *Backyard Hunter: The Praying Mantis*, and Gail Gibbons's *Monarch Butterfly* at the library is a joy. You know your children better than anyone else so you can pick out books that match their interests. The rules are simple.

1. *Follow your child's interests.* If your child likes to play with the computer at school, get books and magazines on computers. If she is interested in bugs, get books on bugs. If she likes to jump rope, get books of jump rope rhymes.

2. *Share books you enjoyed as a child.* If your parents read to you, find the same books to read to your child. There is a special magic in hearing books from the good old days that you read when you were a little girl or boy.

3. *Get a collection of fairy tales.* Look for illustrated versions of individual tales. Interest in fairy tales peaks around seven and eight; children of this age view Hansel and Gretel pushing the witch into

the oven as poetic justice. Their level of morality will change later but this is the last time fairy tales speak to them so clearly.

3. *Find riddle and joke books.* Seven and eight year olds have a weird or "corny" sense of humor. They like elephant jokes, gross punch lines, and jokes that make adults groan. Let them read their jokes aloud to you and try to catch you on the riddles while you're doing the dishes.

4. *Find books about sports stars or heroes.* Have the books available when the hero appears on television so you can capitalize on the current interest by reading more about the person.

5. *Get a craft book.* Make a project together. We once found a book on dinosaurs that had cut-outs for us to make.

6. *Use a cookbook together.* Make a recipe of a favorite food. After you read Laura Ingalls Wilder's *The Little House in the Big Woods*, get *The Little House Cookbook*, which has all the recipes for food mentioned in the series.

7. *Find an interactive book.* Some books allow the reader to make choices about the next section to read, such as the Choose Your Own Adventure books. Let your child read her chosen path to you, then you read your choice to her.

8. *Read to a younger child.* Ask your seven or eight year old to read to a younger child regularly. This additional practice improves their reading fluency and helps them see the joy in sharing books with others.

9. *Find books about things around you.* During the week I spent with our three grandchildren, we took a walk every day because that was one way to

keep them entertained. Because the family lives out in the country, we walked along a not very busy country road taking turns pushing Trisha in her stroller. On the day their parents were coming home, we collected bouquets of weed flowers and wildflowers to fill vases for every room. We found Aliki's book, *A Weed Is a Flower*, to identify the names of the goldenrod, Queen Anne's lace, touch-me-nots, and thistles we had collected.

10. *Make a time capsule for your family.* Use a shoe box or cracker box to prepare a time capsule that tells about your family. Put small objects into the box that when put together reveal important things about your family. You might include photographs, recipes of favorite foods, letters from special people, an unmatched sock, a ribbon or hair clip, some jacks, a ball, an autograph book, a school report, or a drawing.

Making a Writer Out of Your Seven and Eight Year Old

Reading and writing are two sides of the same coin; learning one helps in learning the other. At every developmental level, reading helps writing and writing helps reading. Research shows that writing ability develops side by side with, or even prior to, reading ability. If you ask children entering kindergarten if they know how to read, 90 percent will say, "No." But when you ask the same children if they know how to write, all will say, "Yes."

Even seven- or eight-year-old children do not distinguish totally between drawing and writing to tell a story. They draw pictures, label them, and regard the whole construction as a story. As they develop more control over the ability to express themselves in words, they rely less on illustration and more on words to tell their stories. The more your child writes, the better writer she will be; but she will also become a better reader. Reading a lot makes her a better writer.

Good writers read a lot. They get hunches about how to shape their own ideas from reading the work of other people. In one of Jason's own stories, you can see the influence of both books and first-hand experience. You will also notice some invented spelling — spelling words the way they sound to him, such as characters (caricders) and statue of liberty (stachu of liperte). New approaches to teaching children to write encourage them not to worry about spelling as they get ideas down on paper. Just as real writers go through writing drafts, revising, and editing to get to final copy, so, too, do young children.

Caricders by Jason Russell Ream

One day Cathy was reading a book and all of a sudden the caricders jumped out of the book. And the book was called A Kid's Guide to New York City. And the stachu of liperte was the tallist thing that came out of the book. It walked down the street and some people freaked out because they didn't think the stachu of liperte could walk. All the kids liked the stachu of liperte and they played the hole day with him at the park. The stachu of liperte didn't have his candel lit so a boy went home to get some machts to lite it. And he came back with some machts and lit his candel. After he came down, the stachu of liperte was on fire. They all ran. The fire was so bad that the houses got on fire. And Cathy put the fire out. And everybody said she was a hero. The end.

Jason will eventually learn to spell words correctly as he continues to read, write, and study spelling in school. At this stage, it is important to keep him loving to write instead of insisting on accuracy in spelling. Just as a child learns to read by reading, so does he learn to write by writing. There are many valid reasons for a child to begin writing. Here are some activities that your child can do to make writing real and to make it fun.

Tips for Busy Parents

1. *Write a book about something real or imagined.* Have your child pick a topic. Staple sheets of paper together. Plan how much writing goes on each page. Some children may prefer to compose on the computer. After you print out the story, cut the sections to paste on each page of the book. Have your child illustrate the pages.

2. *Keep a journal.* Encourage your child to write down what she is thinking at the end of each chapter of a book she reads.

3. *Write a thank-you letter.* Whenever Grandma or Aunt Sara remembers a birthday or holiday, ask your child to write them a note to say thanks.

4. *Write your own cards.* Help your child write invitations to her birthday party. Some children

present a book to the school library on their birthday. The librarian has a special bookmark that the child signs and places in the front of the book to identify the donor.

5. *Make your own valentines.* Get red paper, white paper doilies, and glue sticks so your child can create his valentine cards. Elvie Butler has prepared *Celebrate Valentine's Day* to suggest ideas for the holiday.

6. *Keep score at sports events.* Work with your child to keep score at a basketball game or a Little League game. Try to keep the number of points that each player makes.

7. *Write a letter to an author.* Get your child to write a letter to one of her favorite authors. Tell which books she's read and what she thought about them. Tell about herself. Address it to the author at the publisher's address in the book.

8. *Write a letter from one character to another.* Invite your child to write a letter from one of her favorite characters to another. For example, pretend she is Ramona writing to Encyclopedia Brown.

9. *Create a newspaper.* Work with your child to create a family newspaper about your own family. Write feature articles about big family events. Write headlines about family news.

10. *Make a book.* Plan with your child to make a book about your family's history or heritage. Help her to draw a picture of your family tree with spaces for parents, brothers, sisters, grandparents, great-grandparents, aunts, uncles, and cousins. List the dates that members of your family came to America from another country. Make a separate page for each holiday you celebrate and write the things your fam-

ily does to make that day special. List the foods you prepare, the decorations you put up, and the gifts you give. Be sure to include her birthday, Christmas or Hanukkah, Thanksgiving, Halloween, and Valentine's Day. Joan Walsh Anglund has prepared *All About My Family* as a published book in which children can record their family history, place keepsakes, and put family photographs. It is a nice addition or alternate to your own handmade family heritage book.

11. *Write a wish list.* Have your child make a list of the things he wants for his birthday, Christmas, or Hanukkah. Help him to write a letter to Santa or to Grandpa to tell him the things he is hoping for.

12. *Get informational books.* Seven- and eight-year-old children are curious about everything in their world. They want to know how the world works, how things grow, and how their bodies function. Build on this curiosity by giving them informational books that appeal to them. Joanna Cole and Bruce Degen provide some wonderful experiences with science in The Magic School Bus series. *The Magic School Bus at the Waterworks, The Magic School Bus Inside the Earth*, and *The Magic School Bus Inside the Human Body* provide accurate scientific information in a humorous and engaging way. In *The Magic School Bus Lost in the Solar System*, Ms. Frizzle, an unusual teacher, takes her students for a ride they will never forget through the atmosphere and into outer space to land on the moon. In the midst of Ms. Frizzle's explanations, children are acting like children with hilarious side comments and antics. Find books that extend your child's current interests as well as ones to introduce new topics.

13. *Prepare book-related snacks.* When children walk in the door from school, they drop their backpacks and their coats on top of them, then they want a snack. Involve them in preparing healthy snacks and put a poem or book beside them; they will read as they nibble. David McCord's *One at a Time* has many poems about snacks: "Peanut Butter," "Animal Crackers," and "Gingersnaps." He says you can yell for "Bananas and Cream": just say "bananas and scream." He also has poems about radishes, cucumbers, and many other foods. *Brown Bear* health cookies, and *Where the Wild Things Are* wild rice cakes are just the beginning of snack recipes you and your child can create. You can put a note or a poem in his lunchbox; while he eats lunch he will read a gentle reminder of your love.

14. *Start a scrapbook.* Kids are collectors; they'll collect anything from tiny cars to butterflies to stamps to newspaper articles. Let your child choose a subject of interest, get a composition book and a glue stick, and start clipping related news items. Autumn leaves, bird feathers, newspaper articles, and photographs of their favorite sports star all make good scrapbook material. They will read to select items, they will write labels, and they will reread many times as they treasure their collection.

15. *Interview your parents or grandparents.* Help your child make up a list of questions she would like to ask of parents or grandparents. Tape-record the interview so that she can listen again to their comments and stories about what happened when they were her age.

16. *Sketch your family connections.* Use a large sheet of paper to draw connections between several

parts of your family. Work with your child to list aunts, uncles, cousins, and your cousins' cousins.

17. *Explore family letters, albums.* Most people have old packs of letters held together with rubber bands. Allow your child to go through a pack of old letters to see what your family was doing at earlier dates. Maybe there are notes sent when she was born. Encourage her to write a story about what was happening in your family based on the old letters. Go through a family album. Describe family events pictured in the photograph albums.

Surefire Hits for Seven and Eight Year Olds

One of the exciting trends in children's book publishing lies in the production of beautiful informational (or nonfiction) books. Seven and eight year olds are curious about "the olden times when you were a little girl, Mommy." Ann McGovern's *If You Sailed on the Mayflower*, and Ellen Levine's *If You Lived at the Time of Martin Luther King* help you take children back to journey through time. Seymour Simon's science books, Jean Fritz's historical biographies, and Francine Patterson's *Koko's Kitten* satisfy seven and eight year old's endless curiosity and lead them on to new questions.

CHOOSE YOUR OWN ADVENTURE. Almost any of these numerous titles will work. Edward Packard. *The Third Planet from Altair*. Lippincott, 1979; Bantam, 1989.
Children choose a different path each time but end up reading every possible path through the book.

Beverly Cleary. *Ramona Quimby, Age 8*. Morrow, 1981.

Ramona rejoices that she is in the third grade and big enough for her family to depend on.

Joanna Cole. *The Magic School Bus Inside the Earth*. Illustrated by Bruce Degen. Scholastic, 1987.

Ms. Frizzle's class learns firsthand about different kinds of rocks and the formation of the earth from the inside out.

William Cole. *The Square Bear and Other Riddle Rhymes*. Illustrated by Mike Thaler. Scholastic, 1983.

True third-grade humor to make adults groan and children giggle.

Beatrice Schenk de Regniers, editor. *Sing a Song of Popcorn: Every Child's Book of Poems*. Illustrated by nine Caldecott Medal artists. Scholastic, 1988.

A collection of 128 best-loved poems arranged by theme. The work of many poets and award-winning artists provides something for everyone — sheer delight.

Phyllis and Zander Hollander. *Sports Bloopers: Weird, Wacky, and Unexpected Moments in Sports*. Scholastic, 1985.

Lots of mistakes, including running the wrong direction at the Rose Bowl, make this hysterically funny for seven- and eight-year-old sports fans.

Johanna Hurwitz. *The Adventures of Ali Baba Bernstein*. Morrow, 1985; Scholastic, 1987.

David Bernstein finds 17 other people with the

same name so he changes his to Ali Baba. The sequel, *Hurray for Ali Baba Bernstein*, follows David's adventures in the fourth grade.

Barbara Robinson. *The Best Christmas Pageant Ever*. Harper, 1972; Avon, 1973.
　　The worst-behaved kids in town take over all the best parts in the Sunday school Christmas pageant.

Shel Silverstein. *Where the Sidewalk Ends*. Harper, 1974.
　　This book has turned more children on to poetry than perhaps any other book. Verses are outrageous, silly, and sad.

Betty Ren Wright. *The Dollhouse Murders*. Holiday, 1983; Scholastic, 1985.
　　Amy solves a haunting mystery with the help of her family of dolls.

Did You Know . . .

　　Children follow their parents' example. If they see you relax in front of television, they will, too. If they see you read, they will, too.

　　Praise works better than punishment; accentuate the positive things your child does. It helps build self-confidence, which leads to more success.

　　Kids need to know that you are interested in their school. Attend parent meetings, visit your child's classroom. Keep in touch with school.

　　A child will take the same book that was read to him and begin reading it himself.

Ten minutes of freely chosen reading at home makes a big improvement in a child's performance on reading tests at school.

Children learn to become better readers by writing. When children write they notice what other writers do in the books they read.

Children still need to be read to after they learn to read on their own. They need to hear what good reading sounds like.

Chapter 8:
Nine and
Ten Year Olds

Life with Nine and Ten Year Olds

NINE YEAR OLDS

- *Develop best friends*
- *Play sports*
- *Like series books*
- *Like informational books*
- *Are fascinated with strange but true facts*
- *Read* The Guinness Book of World Records
- *Like mysteries*
- *Consider picture books babyish*

- *Prefer tall tales over fairy tales*
- *Like happy endings*
- *Are outgrowing chapter books*
- *Have a weird sense of humor*
- *Like gross, corny jokes*

Eva is nine years old, in the third grade, and has a brother, Philip, who is two years older. Eva is a cat lover. Tigger, her cat, meets her at the door when she comes home from school.

Eva says, "Tigger really counts as a kid. She's the cutest kitten in the whole world." Therefore, Tigger gets the first hug, Mom gets the second. Both hugs occur before Eva drops her backpack, throws her coat on top, and takes off her shoes. Then it's snack-time, talktime to tell Mother all the exciting things that happened at school, and hurry-up time to get ready for the next event.

Eva's life is scheduled five days a week. Monday it's dancing class, Tuesday and Thursday are lessons (religious school), Wednesday it's piano lesson, and Friday it's Brownies. Mom is chauffeur for all events, so they hurry to the car each day. When they return, Eva goes to her room to do her homework. She makes short work of her assignments so she can watch *Duck Tales* and *Tiny Toons* on TV before supper.

Eva says, "After supper, me and Philip jump on my dad and torture him. When Dad gets bored, he sends us to our room. Sometimes I hide under my bed if I'm mad at my parents or want to tease them. Once I put pillows under the covers so they'd think I was in bed."

Eva has lots of friends. She says, "My best friends are Melissa, Lauren, Jamie, Iya, Kyoko, Nachi, and Yuko," proceeding to name every girl in her class at school. "I call them all up on the telephone all the time."

Eva keeps a reading journal for books she reads; she records the title, the author, the date she starts and the date she finishes, the number of pages, and what the book is about. Eva says, "I love Roald Dahl books, series books like the Boxcar Children, Friends 4-Ever, and Sweet Valley Twins and Sweet Valley Kids. Oh, and Laura Ingalls Wilder, she's my favorite. I like really long books." Eva wrote in her autobiography at school:

"Someone special in my life is Omy and Opa. Omy and Opa are very close to me. They are like a third pair of grandparents. Omy makes the best milkshakes in the world. Every time we went to their house, she would ask me what kind of ice cream I wanted and she always had it. Vanilla ice cream. They even had straws called spoon straws; they're little spoons with straws attached to them. Now we don't see Omy and Opa anymore because they moved to Louisiana. I shure do miss them."

TEN YEAR OLDS

- *Are satisfied with themselves*
- *Like adventures with real heroes*
- *Read biographies about real people*
- *Like funny books such as*

How to Eat Fried Worms

- *Enjoy Choose Your Own Adventure-type books*
- *Develop lasting friendships*
- *Play Nintendo and other computer games*
- *Like to watch TV sitcoms and family shows*
- *Enjoy active sports and bike riding*

David is a pet lover; he has 19 pets including fish, hermit crabs, crayfish, newts, and turtles. When he goes to the library, he gets reptile books only. He has read magazines called *Nintendo Power*, and Roald Dahl's books *The Twits* and *James and the Giant Peach*. But he specializes in books about his pets. The big fish tank is in the living room, terrariums are in the dining room and in his room. He feeds his pets before school and helps clean the tanks when they need it.

David's family runs the local Chinese laundry and, every day after school, David and his brother, Sam, go to the laundry. Every Friday, David and Sam go to their grandmother's house in the city and return on Sunday afternoon. David says, "My grandmother fixes me special food like rice, noodles, dumplings, and soup. She tells me stories like 'The Boy Who Cried Wolf,' 'Peter and the Wolf,' and stories about Jesus. I don't know how she remembers everything but she knows 'em all. Nobody reads to me, I can do it myself."

On Wednesday, David has a math tutor and, on

Saturday, he goes to math school close to his grandmother's. David is outstanding in math and says he goes, "Just because my dad wants me to." One time David found that he had left his homework at his home instead of taking it with him to his grandmother's. His older cousin drove out in the middle of the night to retrieve the forgotten homework. There's a great deal of family support to see that David does well, especially in math. When David and Sam are at their grandmother's, they do not go outside to play with neighborhood children. They play with their cousins, watch TV, listen to Grandma's stories, and do homework. Like all children, David is learning his family's values and culture.

Making a Reader Out of Your Nine and Ten Year Old

Nine and ten year olds are active, curious, and full-of-life energy machines. They do not sit around waiting for something to happen; they make things happen so we have to "catch 'em on the run." Your enthusiasm for a project determines the level of your children's interest; if you're excited about it, they will be, too.

Male influences are especially important during these years. Boys use their fathers as role models; girls simply idolize them. If they think Dad is only interested in something you can kick, throw, or catch, that's what they will try to excel in. If they think Dad values reading and education, they will try to excel in those areas.

1. *Take your child to the library.* Show your chil-

dren that you are interested in books, too. Don't just take them to the video store or to the Little League ball field. When children see a parent or older brother or sister checking out books, they will follow the lead.

2. *Get how-to books.* Nine and ten year olds like to be involved in building projects. Get books on how to build a birdhouse, a treehouse, swings, or model airplanes.

3. *Work on building projects together.* Nothing is as rewarding as working on a project with your dad or mom. Building model airplanes is more fun when you work on them together. During the Persian Gulf crisis, sales on model airplanes shot sky high. Everybody wanted to build a Stealth bomber or an F-6 fighter plane. Children can read the instructions as you look over their shoulders. Besides, if they make a mistake, it shows them that it is important to read instructions carefully.

4. *Start a collection.* Nine and ten year olds are collectors. They like baseball cards, NFL player cards, soccer cards. Get books on collecting baseball and football cards. Bruce Brooks, noted author of books for adolescents, is certain that his son learned to read by reading soccer cards. His son, Alexander, memorized players' averages and goal records. Alexander studied the cards, kept them in his room, and carried them with him at all times. He liked to surprise his dad with amazing facts and figures he learned from his soccer cards.

5. *Decorate a T-shirt.* Many people become walking billboards when they put on T-shirts. Make your own using waterproof felt-tipped markers. Create a slogan, a scene, or a caricature of your favorite character. Creativity counts.

6. *Read part of a book aloud.* Get your child started on a book by reading enough of it aloud to get him hooked on the story. Chances are, he'll finish it by himself. I am purposefully using the male pronoun here; it is more often boys than girls at this age who find active sports to fill up their time.

Our son, Jim, was not much of a voluntary reader at age ten. He had to do a book report for school once a month and so he read one book each month — usually the night before the report was due. He always looked for skinny books with lots of pictures. He gave reports on every sports star imaginable because he could use information he gained from the sports pages and TV and really did not have to read the book. He finally did read a book, however; it was *Toward Morning* by Maia Wojciechowska, about the uprising in Poland. He was fascinated by the secret missions young children worked in to undercut the political forces taking over there. The way I got him into that book was to start reading it to him. I read several chapters aloud before he finally said, "Give it to me." He read the rest alone. He used that same book for book reports during the fourth grade, fifth grade, sixth grade, and seventh grade. Today he reads computer magazines, business analyses, and once in a while, a book of political intrigue.

Making a Writer Out of Your Nine and Ten Year Old

Nines and tens have gained reasonable control over the mechanics of writing. They have moved beyond manuscript printing, which they consider babyish, to cursive writing, which they consider quite grown-up. They are able to write for half an hour or more without getting writer's cramp or tired fingers. They see the practical value of writing and will write on their own if it is valued by significant others around them.

1. *Make lists.* Ask your child to write down the items you need from the grocery store by calling them out as you check the cupboards and refrigerator. Here are other lists she can make. Make a list of the relatives who are coming for a holiday so you know how many places to set. Make place cards for a family dinner. Make a list of the friends to be invited to a birthday party. Make a list of all the books you have read together. Make a list about anything; your child enjoys it and gets writing practice.

2. *Make a book.* Some nine and ten year olds help with baby-sitting, especially for younger siblings. Help your son to make an alphabet or counting book to use with the younger child. Make a secret wish book, a grandma book, a grandpa book. Make a shape book — in the shape of a train or van. Make a pop-up book with flaps to lift and figures that raise up. They can use these to entertain younger charges.

3. *Write a letter to an author.* Have your child tell the author what he likes or doesn't like about that author's books. Here is a letter from a fan to Ann M. Martin:

Dear Ms. Martin,
I really like your book *Me and Katie (the Pest)*! It was neat! I like the part when Katie runs away. It was really good. I have read almost all of your Baby-sitters Club books. Are you going to write

more of them? I'm 9 and a half years old. I really like the books you write! My dad told me I have read more books than he has ever read in his life. My mom hopes I keep reading because she says it teaches you new things.

Your friend, Jennifer

4. *Write new verses.* Have your child use a familiar song or tune to write new verses about his family. Use a limerick form of verse to help him write new words, such as "There once was a boy of nine. . . ."

5. *Keep a journal.* Children need to learn that their lives are worth writing about. Keeping a journal about what they do, what they think, how they feel, or what they read is a good way to help them value their own experiences and feel good about themselves. Have them read some autobiographies written by their favorite sports star or author. They find that the simple details about people are very interesting.

Tips for Busy Parents

One summer when Kali and Jason came for their annual visit to Grandma and Grandpa's, we invited Jessica and D. J., a niece and nephew of the same ages. I was shocked to discover that nine-year-old Jessica was a much better reader than ten-year-old Kali. When we read before bedtime, Jessica zoomed through a book while Kali labored over a few pages. One day, I tried an angle that really helped. I read the narrative (the parts that no character said) and had Jessica read the words that one character said and Kali read the dialogue of another character. It worked! We read Lois Lowry's *Anastasia at Your Ser-*

vice and enjoyed the whole experience. Jessica read what Anastasia said and Kali read what her friend said. I read the parts in between. The context or the meaning of the story seemed to carry Kali along. She read the dialogue smoothly and with expression because she understood what was happening in the story.

1. *Read one character's dialogue, have your child read another's.* Children read more easily when what they are reading makes sense to them. Assign or choose parts, let your child become one of the characters and read the words that character says. Some people call this readers' theater. Just have fun and read the parts; it helps bring books and characters to life.

2. *Read riddles.* Nine and ten year olds love to be in on the know. Have them read the riddles and try to outsmart you. Write riddles or make them up for a talking game. I am 5 feet 4 inches tall, have brown hair, and wear glasses. Who am I? Or, I sit on the floor, show pictures, and can flip channels. What am I? I have four wheels, can carry 50 people, and stop frequently. What am I?

3. *Play thinking games.* When you are driving along or preparing a meal, play a guessing game with your child. A simple "Riddle, riddle, ree. I see something you don't see and it begins with 'R' or it used to be called an icebox," is fun and will distract children from horsing around. Twenty questions of animal, vegetable, or mineral works for more mature youngsters. Jeopardy, in which you give the answer and they ask the question, works for even more mature children. Once you start a game, your child will think up variations to make it uniquely yours.

4. *Work on projects.* Kids are continually bringing home projects they need to do. Whether it is for the school science fair, the scouts, or the religion teacher, pitch in and help. This doesn't mean that you do the project for your children but it is more fun for everybody when you get involved. We have helped build volcanoes, carve wooden cars, build model airplanes, create a model of the solar system, and dress a Pilgrim doll, among other things, to get our kids through school.

5. *Support scout activities.* Even if you don't have time to be the Brownie or Cub Scout leader, participate in special events and help at home with scout projects. The Boy Scouts of America and the Girl Scouts of America have created a "Reading Badge." The badge can be earned by reading to people who cannot read, collecting books for people who do not have them, and supporting reading activities in the community.

6. *Write fractured fairy tales.* Nines and tens are a little beyond the traditional fairy tale story. Tell your child to use the stories to write a parody, a new version, a modern news story about the characters, or headlines about the events. Have him write a lost and found column for items found in the fairy tales, such as a spinning wheel, a glass slipper, or a pocketful of crumbs.

7. *Create a camera story.* Photo essays are popular reading material. Children can create their own. Have your child decide on a topic and tell the story in photographs. Of course, Polaroid cameras shorten the waiting time between the idea and the finished product. Nines and tens are not long on patience. Photographs of your child as a baby are immensely

satisfying. Let him use duplicates to create his autobiography in pictures and words.

8. *Write the text for wordless books.* Your child is old enough to create the dialogue for characters in wordless books. Have your child write on little balloons of paper (Post-its work fine) to stick above the characters. Write on strips of paper to attach to each page to tell what is happening in the pictures. You can make a game by keeping the strips loose and using them to match up to the right picture. Mercer Mayer, Fernando Krahn, and John Goodall create fascinating wordless books. If you buy wordless books in paperback, cut up a copy and see if your child can put it back in order — in proper sequence. It's all fun and you can make it more fun if you buy two copies, paste each page on construction paper, and ask your child to recreate the story sequence. Some people object to cutting up a book even though children use it many times. If this bothers you, use comic strips from the newspaper to cut into segments. Children can put them in sequence.

Surefire Hits for Nine and Ten Year Olds

Judy Blume. *Tales of a Fourth Grade Nothing.* Dutton, 1972; Dell, 1986.

Peter considers himself a fourth-grade nothing but his pet turtle, Dribble, is important to him. Fudge, Peter's two-and-a-half-year-old brother, creates trouble for everybody, including Dribble.

Roald Dahl. *James and the Giant Peach.* Illustrated

by Nancy Ekholm Burket. Knopf, 1961; Penguin, 1988.

James, an orphan, is miserable with Aunts Sponge and Spiker; he leaves his mean relatives and escapes to a new home inside a giant peach.

Jean Fritz. *What's the Big Idea, Ben Franklin?* Putnam, 1982.

One of several biographies Fritz has written about heroes during the Revolutionary War period. The books are filled with personal detail and humorous facts to help readers know the people as real life human beings.

Deborah and James Howe. *Bunnicula: A Rabbit Tale of Mystery.* Atheneum, 1979; Avon, 1980.

Harold the dog tells the story of the Monroe family who have Chester the cat and a newcomer bunny they name Bunnicula, after Dracula. Chester thinks Bunnicula is really a vampire and tries to communicate his suspicions to the humans. Sequels continue the humorous animal stories.

X. J. Kennedy and Dorothy Kennedy. *Knock at a Star: A Child's Introduction to Poetry.* Illustrated by Karen Weinhaus. Little, Brown, 1983.

This book tells what poems do and the forms poems take. Examples of each type help children understand and enjoy poetry.

Patricia MacLachlan. *Sarah, Plain and Tall.* Harper, 1985, 1987.

Anna and Caleb live with their father in a sod house on the prairie in the late 1800s. When their father advertises for a mail order bride, they fear the worst but hope for the best.

Shel Silverstein. *The Light in the Attic.* Harper, 1981.
This is the book guaranteed to turn your children into poetry lovers. Silverstein's oddball humor in verses and drawings make readers laugh or gasp with surprise. The book was on the best-seller list for 188 weeks, longer than any other book since the list began.

E. B. White. *Charlotte's Web.* Illustrated by Garth Williams. Harper, 1952.
The classic story of a spider, Charlotte, who spins words into her web to rescue the impetuous but lovable pig, Wilbur.

Laura Ingalls Wilder. *The Little House in the Big Woods.* Illustrated by Garth Williams. Harper, 1953, 1986.
Laura tells the story of her own life in the log cabin in Wisconsin during the 1870s. Eight sequels continue Laura Ingalls Wilder's story.

Did You Know . . .

Children like to read what *they* choose to read — not what others choose for them.
Children will read magazine articles on topics that interest them. Those interested in animals read nature magazines; those interested in computers read *Nintendo Power.*
Children in grades three through twelve learn the

114

meanings of about 3,000 new words a year — the majority of new words are learned incidentally while reading books and other materials.

Voracious readers are made, not born. No child is born loving baseball or pizza; they learn to like what they see their parents valuing.

Children who read most, also read best, according to national tests of reading ability.

Most avid readers go through a stage of reading "series" books. Although the series may not qualify as "good" literature, all that reading practice helps develop speed and fluency.

Research shows that if there is time for reading in school, kids will also read at home. See if your school allows time for independent reading.

Chapter 9:
Eleven and
Twelve Year Olds

Life with Eleven and Twelve Year Olds

ELEVEN YEAR OLDS

- *Like boys (girls), and like girls (boys)*
- *Listen to rap music and rock music*
- *Like to dance to rap music, e.g., L.L. Cool J*
- *Like horror movies and stories*
- *Like Nancy Drew mysteries*
- *Like series books, (Babysitter's Club, Sweet Valley High)*

- *Find that friends are very important*
- *Want their hair to be perfect and clothes to be in fashion*
- *Like babies and little kids*
- *Talk on the telephone as much as allowed*
- *Write notes to friends*
- *Memorize poetry and song lyrics*
- *Like to ice skate, roller skate*
- *Like basketball, football, baseball, all sports*
- *Read teenage magazines (Creem, Guitar Player, Propaganda)*
- *Like animals and animal stories, particularly horse stories*
- *Like survival and adventure stories*
- *Like happy endings to stories*
- *Imitate their friends in dress and behavior*
- *Begin an interest in science fiction*
- *Read about people just a little older than they are*

"I cleaned my eleven-year-old son's room the other night and noticed a little spiral notebook I had gotten him to keep his assignments in," says Linda, a mother in DeKalb, Illinois. "The notebook was filled so I asked him if he needed a new one and he said, 'I didn't really use it for that. Go ahead and look at what I did use it for.' The notebook didn't have any assignments written in it beyond the first two pages but he had written other things so I started reading.

"He had copied down tidbits of poetry by Yeats, lyrics from Billy Joel, Paul Simon, the Rolling Stones, and the Grateful Dead songs, and a few poems from a book by Mel Glenn. I was fascinated so I kept reading. I found some poems that were not credited to any poet so I asked him, 'Who wrote these?' His answer, 'I did,' astounded me. I had no idea that he was interested in reading poetry let alone that he was trying to write poetry."

Megan, my eleven-year-old goddaughter, took me into her room during a recent visit. I noticed stacks of paperback books spilling out from her bedside table. Closer inspection showed me that Megan was reading every series going. There were Sweet Valley High, Sweet Valley Twins, The Baby-sitters Club, Bad News Ballet, The Boxcar Children, Dear Diary, Friends 4-Ever, The Gymnasts, and Sleepover Friends.

I commented, "Oh, I see you like to read series books." Megan answered, "Yeah, I do." Her mother followed us into the room and said, "We just finished reading Katherine Paterson's *Bridge to Terabithia*." Megan retorted, "Yeah, and if you ever make me read another book like that that makes me cry, I'll never read again. And you better not make me read any books where an animal gets killed either." Megan, like many other eleven year olds, still wants happy endings and an ideal world portrayed in the books she reads for pleasure.

TWELVE YEAR OLDS

- *Like rap, rock and roll, and heavy metal music*
- *Participate in all kinds of sports*
- *Begin to specialize in some sport*
- *Like physical activity*
- *Eat like a horse, a bottomless pit*
- *Show interest in the opposite sex*
- *Begin informally dating, mostly in groups*
- *Read fashion, rock music, and teenage magazines*
- *Like American history in fact and fiction*
- *Like horror stories and movies*
- *Like comedy, fantasy, and science fiction*
- *Watch TV sitcoms from thirty minutes to six hours a day*
- *Are very interested in their social life*
- *Are interested in makeup, clothes, hairstyles (girls)*

- *Are interested in clothes and hairstyles (boys)*
- *Spend endless hours on the telephone with friends*
- *Have mood swings; seem grown-up one minute, a child the next*
- *Like to do things for themselves*
- *Like to be cool*

Jared, in the sixth grade, is a black belt, first degree, in karate. On Monday, he teaches karate to younger children. On Tuesday, he goes to karate lessons. On Wednesday, he goes to Hebrew School. On Thursday, he goes to karate lessons. On Friday, he teaches another class in karate. Needless to say, karate is important to Jared and his family. Furthermore, Jared reads nonfiction karate books.

The girls in Jared's classroom consider him a "hunk." The boys turn to him as a leader in sports, dress, hairstyles, and behavior. His teacher, Ed Conti, says, "Fortunately, Jared is a good kid." Jared comes to the schoolyard to play sports before or after his karate sessions. He tells disapprovingly about some kids who blew up their family mailbox with firecrackers last Fourth of July. Jared's big brother is his model; he has inherited lots of his big brother's clothes and his values. Jared chooses to read karate books primarily, but when Mr. Conti read aloud from Gary Paulsen's *Hatchet*, Jared got the book and read ahead on his own. Like many other twelve-year-old boys, Jared is interested in many things; he follows up on books that strike his interests.

Michael, a sixth-grader in a small school, is a bright young boy talented in basketball, baseball, soccer, judo, wrestling, and dancing. His interest in reading for pleasure is absolute zero. Zilch! Each month, Michael has a book report due for school but weeks pass and he doesn't read the book. When his mother asks why, he says, "Because I hate to read." Michael's mother, Susan, tells us what happened to bring this about.

"When Michael was five, he asked me, 'When will I learn to read?' I told him, 'When you go to school.' I encouraged him to follow the words as I read and I asked people how I could teach my son to read. His kindergarten teacher said, 'Just read to him.' This was frustrating to me because Michael wanted to read so badly and I didn't know how to teach him.

"In the first grade, Michael had a nice grandmotherly type teacher. She had her hands full with eleven squirmy, active boys in her classroom. Her first remark to me at his conference was, 'Michael is a lovely boy, but . . . he has ants in his pants.' He was put in the lowest reading group and remained there until second grade when things got worse.

"After the first spelling test in second grade, Michael came home happily and said excitedly, 'Guess what, Mommy! I only have to write two sentences from now on. The rest of the kids have to do five.' In the second half of second grade, Michael was tested for a learning disability.

"Michael spent third grade leaving the classroom for the remediation and resource room five days a week during regular school time. When he left, the class proceeded in a normal manner, which left him out of certain things. During these years I continued to read to Michael at home while I read to my younger daughter. Michael seemed to get bored with the stories his little sister wanted to hear so I would read to them separately.

"In the fourth grade, Michael had an inspiring teacher. She was energetic, enthusiastic, and read to her students every day. They were free to speak their viewpoints and make comments about the books. She varied the homework each night and assigned one book report each week. Since the children loved her, they were as enthusiastic to read as she was. Michael came home one day and told me that he knew how to get an A on his next paper. He said with enthusiasm, 'You just put more stuff in it!' His desire to read increased at this point. His writing became clearer and there were no more problems about doing his homework.

"Fifth grade was not a problem as I saw it but I don't think Michael's teacher was strict or demanding. He completed all his homework but reading real books was not a part of the school day.

"Now in sixth grade, Michael was assigned to read a historical fiction book. Since I've been learning about children's books, I knew which one to get. I went to the library alone since Michael doesn't want to go anymore and took out the book, *Number the Stars*, a Newbery winner. The book sat on his dresser for four days. Every day I asked him if he was going to read it and he would say yes but never read the book. The fact that he was so turned off to reading and said he hated it had been bothering me for a long time. I had to change this.

"One evening I asked Michael if he wanted me to read to him. He looked at me as if I were crazy. I told him he was never too old to enjoy being read to; in fact, I still enjoy it. He thought for a moment and then said, 'I don't care.' Well, I *did* care so I took his answer as a yes and we started the book. We read one chapter a night; sometimes he asked for more and I read more. Do you know that he gave me a break, too? I never asked him to read but he volunteered. When he read, he read with expression and enthusiasm. The book was interesting to him. He wrote a wonderful book report and was very proud of himself.

"Michael and I still read together because finishing one book did not totally change his way of thinking but it was a start. I like being a reading partner to a child who *hates* to read but who loves to be read to. I know that one day he'll discover that reading is fun and has nothing to do with those boring books and ditto sheets from school. I just think it's sad that he missed so many years of good reading."

Making a Reader Out of Your Eleven and Twelve Year Old

Eleven and twelve year olds have minds of their own; they think they are much more independent than they really are. It is frightening to realize that as parents we will soon have even less influence over their decisions than we have now. It is also frightening to know that outside demands on their time will increase as they move into the teenage years.

This is a period for a last ditch effort to turn children into readers.

Some say that if children are not readers by the time they leave elementary school, they probably will never become avid readers. I don't exactly agree with this dire prediction but I will say that if children never read or hear a really *good* book by the time they are teenagers, they're not likely to become readers.

The man who cuts my hair, Marcello, has a twelve-year-old son. Just as I do with anyone I talk with for more than three minutes, I asked if his son was a reader. He said, "No, Dino is more interested in playing sports and horsing around than in reading. He only reads what he has to read for school." This was a challenge I couldn't refuse. I took Robert Cormier's book, *The Chocolate War*, with me on my next visit to Marcello. He seemed embarrassed but said he would try it with Dino. I have this much faith in Cormier's book! I knew that if his father read the book to him, Dino would at least try another book.

Weeks passed. Each time I went to the hairdresser, I asked if he had started the book yet. Each time the answer was no, there wasn't time. Finally I told the hairdresser that I was writing about him and Dino; I couldn't finish my book if he didn't start to read. He said, "I'll see what we can do. We're going to Italy this summer and that book will be good to read on our seven-hour flight." I know that I'm putting pressure on my barber; he may read the book just to shut me up. But if he does and if Dino finds out that great stories come from books, well, that'll be one for our side, won't it?

Elevens and twelves believe their friends and their teachers more readily than they believe their parents.

If a friend says a book is good, then it must be good. If a teacher reads aloud from a book at school, they want to get the book to read ahead, to follow along, or to reread the same book.

Pre-teens are social animals. They run in packs. They imitate their friends. They want to be cool. They want to look like everybody else and do not want to stand out in a crowd in any way. Their clothes, their hairstyles, and the books they read must assure them they are one of the "in" group.

1. *Give a friend a book.* Give your child's friend a book you want your child to read. This may not be a very subtle move but it works.

2. *Send a book to the teacher.* If you know a book children of this age should read, send it to the teacher with a request that it be read aloud to the group. Chances are that your child will want a copy, too.

3. *Subscribe to a teenage magazine.* Children want to read above their age level. They like to read about people just a couple of years older than they are. Teen magazines are just right. Children read them to practice what they will be like in a few years.

4. *Get books about their hero.* Sports figures, dancers, musicians, rock stars, TV stars, movie stars, authors, poets, scientists, Stormin' Norman Schwarzkopf, General Colin Powell, and other modern day heros appear in books. Find the books at the library and sprinkle them in your pre-teenager's path.

5. *Start your child on series books.* When children read the first book in a series, they are anxious to find the second one. Nancy Drew, Sweet Valley Twins, Baby-sitter's Club and Friends 4-Ever are all fair

game. Reading books in a series increases the amount a child reads, which increases fluency, comprehension, and vocabulary.

6. *Read a book to your child.* Elevens and twelves are not too old to be read to. Choose a book you have heard about and say, "I've been wanting to read this book. How about if we read it together? I'll start."

7. *Find movies based on books.* Modern pre-teens like going to the movies. *The Black Stallion; The Call of the Wild; All Things Bright and Beautiful; Sarah, Plain and Tall;* and many other books have been made into films. Once children have seen the movie, they'll want to read the book.

8. *Find music to accompany reading.* Ask your child to select music to go along with a story or verses. Set verses to rap music.

9. *Create a literary jackdaw.* A jackdaw is named for the bird that collects all sorts of objects in its nest. Help your child make a literary jackdaw by having him collect objects related to a book and putting them in a box. The items serve as an excellent way to give a report on a book.

Making a Writer Out of Your Eleven and Twelve Year Old

Young people of eleven and twelve can easily see through attempts to get them to write for the sake of writing. Make writing projects practical and meaningful. Adults write for real reasons and pre-teens will write for reasons meaningful to them. Try to adapt writing needs to their interests and activities.

1. *Prepare a baby-sitter's kit.* Many elevens and twelves baby-sit for young children. Help your children to prepare a kit they take with them on baby-sitting jobs. Ask them to make a list of basic safety rules, steps to take in an emergency, and ways to entertain their charges.

2. *Write lyrics for a popular melody.* Encourage your child to use the characters and plot of a book as the basis for the lyrics to one of her favorite tunes or melodies.

3. *Make a literary map.* Use one story, such as Tolkien's *Lord of the Rings*, as the basis for the map. Get your pre-teens to draw a map of the territory the characters travel. Have them make a map of the world to record the setting of all the books they have read.

4. *Write a review.* Pre-teens like to know that their opinions are valued. Get them to review books for their friends or for a review journal that publishes adolescents' reviews.

5. *Make a crossword puzzle.* Suggest that your child use the characters, objects, and events in a book as the basis for a crossword puzzle. Make a standard crossbreak diagram. Start filling in words from the book. Make up clues for the words.

6. *Create a time-line.* Time-lines help young people put events into chronological sequence. Show your child how to use the time-line for her own life, the works of one author, or historical events and related books. A time-line of the books a child read at various ages is interesting and shows how much reading tastes change over the years.

7. *Make an acrostic.* Show your child how to write the title of a book down the side of a page along the margin. For each letter in the title, give a word that

describes her feelings about the book, or give the name of a character, place, or event which figures in the book. Another possibility is to write a sentence that begins with each letter of the title.

8. *Write a picture book.* The story in picture books is told through a combination of words and illustrations. Help your child to create a picture book to put into the baby-sitter's kit. Decide which words go on each page and illustrate the story. He can expand the story told in words by weaving a subplot into the illustrations. Hide objects in the illustrations for younger children to find; young children like hidden pictures.

9. *Write a sequel.* Follow a favorite character from a story by writing additional episodes with your child. Tell the story from a minor character's point of view. Move backward or forward in time to tell what is happening to the characters. Set the story in a new setting, for example, your neighborhood. Add a new character to a story. For example, the fourth little pig is a girl who huffs and puffs and blows the brick house down. She asks why the three little pigs want to sit at home and miss all the fun and excitement going on out in the world.

10. *Write a parody.* Show your child how to use a familiar folktale as the basis for a parody, a comic imitation of a well-known piece of literature. Look at the books *Deep in the Forest*, *Jim and the Beanstalk*, and *The Jolly Postman* for examples of parodies.

11. *Write a poem from a name.* Write your child's or another's name down the side of a page. Together think of words to describe the person. Here's one that one of my students wrote:

B is for Brenda, black, beautiful, bright
R is for reading and running all right
E is for experience, extending my reach
N is for nursery school I want to teach
D is for dancing and digging each day
A is for ambitious, 'cause that's my way.

Tips for Busy Parents

Pre-teens are rather independent. They like to do things for themselves and swing from totally responsible, mature individuals to pouting, demanding, immature wimps. If you turn your child into a reader now you will make life easier for yourself and your child in the future.

1. *Put a book in your child's room.* This is tempting by tantalizing. If a new book is lying there, chances are that your child will take a look at it.

2. *Tell about a book you enjoyed.* Find a book you enjoyed as a teenager or pre-teen. Read parts aloud to give your child a taste or flavor of the book. Read enough of it to tempt your child to read the rest of it.

3. *Start your child on a new series.* Reading series books is like eating peanuts; you can't stop with one. When children read from a series they know who the characters are, what to expect in the plot, and how it will probably turn out. They read fast, develop fluency, and increase their vocabulary. They pick up the reading habit. They will move on toward more sophisticated books as their reading habit grows and they find reading is fun to do. See John Christopher, Helen Cresswell, Ursula LeGuin, C. S. Lewis, Lois

Lowry, L. M. Montgomery, Richard Peck, and Cynthia Voigt for outstanding series books.

Surefire Hits for Eleven and Twelve Year Olds

Lloyd Alexander. *The Book of Three*. Holt, 1964; Dell, 1978.

Taran, an Assistant Pig Keeper, faces villains in his search for his true identity. The fantasy, based on Welsh folklore, shows Taran's initiation into heroism. This is the first book in a series of five. Once started, your child will read them all.

Judy Blume. *Are You There, God? It's Me, Margaret*. Bradbury, 1970; Dell, 1972.

Margaret and her friends worry about developing bosoms and starting their menstrual period. Margaret talks to God about religion, loyalty, and family relationships.

Robert Cormier. *The Chocolate War*. Pantheon, 1974; Dell, 1986.

Jerry's school sponsors a sale of chocolate bars but Jerry decides he does not want to participate. The pressure to conform leads Jerry to ask, "Do I dare disturb the universe?"

Jean Craighead George. *Julie of the Wolves*. Harper, 1972.

Julie, a young Eskimo girl, faces life alone on the frozen tundra. She survives only by making friends with a wolf pack.

Scott O'Dell. *Island of the Blue Dolphins*. Houghton Mifflin, 1960; Dell, 1987.

Based on the true experiences of a native girl on an island off the coast of California. Karana is marooned on the island when she swims back to rescue her younger brother. Eventually, Karana faces a solitary life and uses skills her forebears taught her.

Katherine Paterson. *Bridge to Terabithia*. Crowell, 1977; Harper, 1987.

Jesse and Leslie develop an unlikely friendship and create an imaginary kingdom they call Terabithia. Jesse must deal with Leslie's untimely death and his grief by passing on Leslie's gift of imagination to his little sister.

Marjorie Kinnan Rawlings. *The Yearling*. Scribner's, 1962; Macmillan, 1988.

A young boy in the Florida swamplands raises a pet deer. His sacrifice of the deer is heartbreakingly tender.

Wilson Rawls. *Where the Red Fern Grows*. Doubleday, 1961, 1973.

Billy Colman raises two hound puppies to be hunting dogs in his mountain area homeland. The dogs' unbridled loyalty to Billy and to each other leads to tragedy and heartache. Dog lovers are guaranteed to cry.

Mildred Taylor. *Roll of Thunder, Hear My Cry*. Dial, 1976; Puffin, 1991.

Cassie Logan and her family face discrimination and racial hatred in their Southern community. The love that binds the family is heartwarming. Continue reading about the Logan family in *Song of the Trees* (a prequel), *Friendship*, *Let the Circle Be Unbroken*, and *The Road to Memphis*.

Cynthia Voigt. *Homecoming*. Atheneum, 1981.

Thirteen-year-old Dicey leads two younger brothers and a sister to safety after their mother abandons them in a shopping center. Dicey knows the children will be split up into foster homes if she waits for help. Instead of waiting she leads them to a new home. You can continue the series about the Tillerman family in *Dicey's Song, The Runner, Come a Stranger,* and *Solitary Blue.*

Did You Know . . .

If the adults in the home don't read, the children are not likely to pick up the reading habit.

Children will read a book that a friend recommends more quickly than one an adult recommends.

Something magical happens when a child reads the right book at the right time. If a child finds that a character in a book suffers from the same fears as her own, then she knows that she is not alone.

Students who have the biggest vocabulary are the best readers. If you want to know how well a child will read, find out how many words he knows.

Children learn to become better readers by reading. No matter what they read, the additional practice makes them good at what they do.

Reading helps to develop the imagination. No new

inventions would ever be created without imagination.

Pre-teens and teenagers still need to hear someone
read aloud. Find interesting bits in newspapers or
magazines that you can read aloud while they are
cleaning up after a meal.

We should share our reading secrets with kids. Let
them know that you sometimes skip a chapter,
sneak a peek at the ending, skip a word you don't
know.

Not all books are good books for everyone. Let your
child develop his own taste for the types of books
and magazines he reads.

Chapter 10:
A Final Word

As I was completing the manuscript for this book, an article appeared in the local newspaper that made me think I had skipped a very important part of reading aloud — the joy that comes to the reader! The article describes a project in Bridgeport, Connecticut, in which the School Volunteer Association organizes more than 500 people to visit individual classes in virtually every school to read for an hour and then to donate the books to the school. Even the Mayor pulls up a child-sized chair and reads to rapt listeners.

The teachers noticed that children were reading more books on their own than they ever had before the project started. One veteran teacher said, "I'm convinced it's due to Read Aloud."

We know this is the case. Children want to read on their own the books they've heard read aloud. But the article went on to describe another result of the project: the effect on the people who do the reading aloud. Every week, bank employees hurry to jump in their cars to commute to their adopted school. Each banker carries a new book bought by the bank, plus some personally purchased treats. One worker, Ms. Kelly, from the commercial mortgage department says, "I walk into the school full of hopes every time, and I walk out wondering why I'm working in a bank and not at this school." Ms. Kelly went on to say, "I told my boss he moves a lot slower than these little people. You blink and they go from here to there. Their enthusiasm is so intoxicating. *They* end up telling *me* stories."

Other workers noticed the good feelings Ms. Kelly talked about so they were curious and signed up to join the Read Aloud team.

Tina Ladnier said, "You walk in the classroom after a difficult morning at work, and every single young-ster yells, 'Hi, Tina!' and, boom, you're right back up. They remember every book I've read them. And they write poems just for me. I'm sentimental, but I'm afraid I get more from this than they do."

Word has gotten around at the bank. There's a waiting list of adults eager to read to the enthusiastic children. The project has also grown beyond reading aloud. The bankers helped to build a new playground at the school, students visited the bank's computer center, and students followed their readers around while they were at work for a day. One banker prom-ised to bring something special for Show and Tell: her fiancé. Reading aloud works its magic in both directions — from the person who reads aloud to children then it comes back doublefold to the reader.

I learned about the effects of reading aloud as I read to my own children. I didn't have the research evidence then, just my own hunches. Years later I read about a man in England, Gordon Wells, who provided the research evidence. In order to study what makes a difference in children's lives, he "bugged" a large number of them, with parents' permission, of course. He hooked little microphones onto them to click on automatically at various times during the day so he could count the times the child had anything to do with reading or writing. It might be a parent at the grocery store saying, "Get the box that says cornflakes." Or it might be reading a story to the child, writing a letter to Grandma, or putting magnetic letters on the refrigerator.

Wells kept track of the daily events connected to reading or writing in the children's lives from the time they were fifteen months until they were just over five years old. At one extreme there was Jonathan who had over 5,000 experiences with print, and at the other end Rosie who had none.

On school entrance tests, Jonathan scored at the top and Rosie scored at the bottom. Wells continued to keep track of the children throughout their elementary school years. Sad but true, Jonathan was still at the top on school tests and Rosie was still at the bottom after five years of schooling.

Wells explains the difference between the children's lives and says, unquestionably, it was the sharing of stories that was most important. He found that children need stories because they use them to make sense of their own lives. The many stories Jonathan heard helped him to understand his own world in a way that Rosie could never know.

My years as a teacher, mother, and now grandmother have shown me what loving to read does for a child. Children who read are confident, alert, and in charge of their world. They don't need to depend on others to do their thinking for them; they can find out what they want to know by themselves. The feelings of independence and self-esteem make a marked difference in children assuming responsibility for their actions and in shaping their attitude toward life. Good books may not save the world but they are one of the reasons the world is worth saving.

Now I, too, know the importance of reading to children and can share that knowledge with other parents. "Please read to me" is more than a child's request for attention, it's an opportunity to expand a child's mind. The joy goes in both directions, so be prepared to enjoy the process yourself.

Michael Ende, in *The Neverending Story*, says that our fantasies and fairy tale characters will die if we don't tell their stories. The lines between fantasy and reality are blurred; fantasy is in danger of being lost forever. Our ability to imagine, and the world of make believe, will not exist unless we keep it alive by passing it on to children. This is a part of our legacy to children; surely they deserve to hear the myths and legends that have been passed down to us. If our legends die, the world will be a less interesting place to be.

Growing up on a farm kept me close to nature and the basic qualities of life. It taught me that important things worth having were worth working for and worth waiting for. The trees I helped plant as a child are sturdy and huge now; they give shade to others who farm the land. I remember the slender little saplings we planted and watered and nurtured and put stakes around so the cows wouldn't trample them. We took care of them because we cared about them. When I read *The Little Prince* I found that Antoine de Saint-Exupéry had said long ago that we are responsible for the things we raise. Our children are the most beautiful legacy we will ever have.

Each time you read a story to your child, you are planting a seed and nurturing it. Each time you use an activity found here — or one of your own — that involves children in reading or writing, you are helping your child learn to love books. Congratulations on what you have done thus far. You've already learned that the joy you give returns to you a hundred fold; it keeps on growing. That's the beauty of planting seeds! I hope you raise a beautiful garden of readers to make the world a more beautiful place.

Appendix

Children's Magazines

When you choose a magazine, ask yourself these questions:

Is the magazine right for my child's age and interests?

Does it have an appealing format and design?

Is the quality worth the price?

Ages Two to Twelve. Preschool through Grade Six

Highlights for Children. A 42-page, full-color, general interest magazine with original stories, articles, hidden pictures, activities, puzzles, Timbertoes, and Goofus and Gallant. Designed to help children grow in basic skills, knowledge, creativity, sensitivity to others, and the ability to think and reason. Order: Highlights for Children, Inc., 2300 West Fifth Avenue, Columbus, OH 43272-0002.

Cricket. An 80-page literary magazine with literature, nature, science, history, astronomy, art, music, sports, crafts, cartoons, and puzzles. Intended to create a love of reading, appreciation for good writing and illustration, and an understanding of cultural values of all people. Order: Cricket Magazine, P. O. Box 51144, Boulder, CO 80321-1144. (Also order: Carus Publishing Company, P. O. Box 300, Peru, IL 61354.)

Ages 4 to 9. Preschool to Primary Grades

Chickadee. A 32-page, "hands on," science and nature magazine intended to interest children in their environment and the world around them. Stories, crafts, puzzles, science experiments, and articles on animals and nature. Order: Young Naturalist Foundation, 56 The Esplanade, Suite 306, Toronto, Ontario M5E 1A7, Canada. (416) 868-6001.

Ladybug. A 40-page, full-color, collection of stories, games, and educational activities aimed at creating a love of reading, developing imagination and sensibilities, and encouraging read-aloud sessions in families. Order: Cricket Country Lane, Box 50284,

Boulder, CO 80321-0284. (800) 284-7257, ext. 4L. (Also order: Carus Publishing Company, P. O. Box 300, Peru, IL 61354.)

Sesame Street. A 32-page, full-color, general interest magazine designed to educate and entertain while helping preschoolers make the transition from television to printed material. Activities, articles, and stories on people from many cultures, careers. Order: Children's Television Workshop, One Lincoln Plaza, New York, NY 10023.

Ages Seven to Twelve. Grades Two to Six

National Geographic World. A 32–36 page, full-color magazine designed to provide geographic information, to open windows to the world, and to stimulate creative thinking and activity. Outdoor adventure, natural history, science, astronomy, social science, sports, games, crafts, and puzzles. Order: National Geographic Society, Dept 00789, 17th and M. St. N. W., Washington, DC 20036. (Also order: National Geographic World, P. O. Box 2330, Washington, DC 20077-9955.)

Ranger Rick. A 48-page, full-color, natural history magazine devoted to inspiring an understanding and appreciation of the natural world and environmental issues. Animals, nature, science, astronomy, and activities. Order: National Wildlife Federation, 8925 Leesburg Pike, Vienna, VA 22184.

Sports Illustrated for Kids. A 76-page, full-color,

collection of articles on professional, amateur, and youth sports planned to increase information and participation in athletics. Articles about sports events, sports stars, good food, exercise, playing skills, rules, and equipment. Order: Sports Illustrated for Kids, Time Inc. Magazine Company, Time & Life Building, Rockefeller Center, New York, NY 10020-1393. (Also order: Sports Illustrated for Kids, P. O. Box 830607, Birmingham, AL 35283-0607.)

3-2-1 Contact. A 44-page, full-color, science magazine intended to show how technology and science can be fun and accessible to all. Articles on science, environment, health, medicine, math, computers, psychology, and sociology. Order: Children's Television Workshop, One Lincoln Plaza, New York, NY 10023. (Also order: P. O. Box 53051, Boulder, CO 80322-53051.)

Cobblestone: The History Magazine for Young People. A 48-page, black-and-white and color-history magazine. Each issue focuses on a theme dealing with an aspect of American history. Articles, stories, photo essays, crafts, maps, time-lines, recipes, and activities. Order: Cobblestone Publishing, Inc., 30 Grove Street, Peterborough, NH 03458.

*U*S* Kids.* A 40-page, full-color, general interest magazine intended to increase children's interest in learning about themselves and their world. Stories, articles, activities, and the Puzzle Squad adventures. Order: Field Publications, 245 Long Hill Road, Middletown, CT 06457.

*   *   *

Zillions. A 32-page, full-color, consumer-education magazine designed to provide unbiased consumer information. Aimed at improving children's decision-making and consumer skills. (Previously named *Penny Power.*) Order: Consumers Union, 256 Washington Street, Mount Vernon, NY 10553.

Odyssey. A 40-page, black-and-white and full-color astronomy magazine designed to spark interest in space exploration. Each issue focuses on a specific theme. Original articles on space, astronomy, NASA, observatories, and a robot named Ulysses 4—11. Order: Cobblestone Publishing, Inc., 30 Grove Street, Peterborough, NH 03458.

Surefire Hits: Extended Booklist

Preschoolers

Eric Carle. *The Very Hungry Caterpillar*. Philomel, 1981.

On each day of the week, a caterpillar eats his way through a number of food items until he has a tummyache, turns into a cocoon, and emerges as a beautiful butterfly. See also *The Very Quiet Cricket* and *The Very Busy Spider*.

Tomie dePaola. *Tomie dePaola's Mother Goose*. Putnam, 1985.

Over 200 Mother Goose nursery rhymes charmingly illustrated in full color by a world renowned artist.

Jakob and Wilhelm Grimm. *Little Red Riding Hood.* Illustrated by Trina Schart Hyman. Holiday House, 1982.

Trina Schart Hyman adds the right amount of mystery, scariness, and warmth to her illustrations and retelling of the old fairy tale.

Deborah Guarino. *Is Your Mama a Llama?* Illustrated by Steven Kellogg. Scholastic, 1989.

Lloyd the llama asks each animal in turn until he finds his own mother. With rhyming text and a guessing game format, a wonderful read-aloud.

Vera Williams. *"More More More," Said the Baby: Three Love Stories.* Greenwillow, 1990.

Grown-ups express joy and love for a child, in three multiethnic families.

Audrey Wood. *The Napping House.* Illustrated by Don Wood. Harcourt Brace Jovanovich, 1984.

In cumulative fashion, a snoring granny, a dreaming child, a dozing dog, a snoozing cat, and a slumbering mouse go to sleep but awaken when a wakeful flea takes a bite.

Five and Six Year Olds

Karen Ackerman. *Song and Dance Man.* Illustrated by Stephen Gammell. Knopf, 1988.

A loving grandfather, a retired vaudeville performer, takes his grandchildren up rickety attic steps to recreate for them scenes from his old song-and-dance routines.

Janet and Allan Ahlberg. *The Jolly Postman and Other People's Letters*. Little, Brown, 1986.
The jolly postman delivers actual letters, postcards, and invitations from one storybook character to another. Try to keep the separate pieces in the envelopes for the next reading.

Margaret Wise Brown. *Goodnight Moon*. Illustrated by Clement Hurd. Harper, 1947.
The perfect bedtime story about a rabbit child saying goodnight to all the things in his room as he watches the moon travel across the sky outside his window.

Stephanie Calmenson. *The Principal's New Clothes*. Illustrated by Denise Brunkus. Scholastic, 1989.
A hilarious twist on *The Emperor's New Clothes* — the school principal is tricked into wearing just his underwear to school!

Mary Ann Hoberman. *A House Is a House for Me*. Illustrated by Betty Fraser. Viking, 1978.
Rhythmic verse creates images of all the things that serve as "houses" for objects and ideas; such as a book is a house for a story.

Bill Martin, Jr. *Polar Bear, Polar Bear, What Do You Hear?* Illustrated by Eric Carle. Henry Holt, 1991.
The lilting question-and-answer cumulative pattern that children can read on their own after hearing

it once or twice. See also *Brown Bear, Brown Bear, What Do You See?*

Trinka Hakes Noble. *The Day Jimmy's Boa Ate the Wash.* Illustrated by Steven Kellogg. Dial, 1980.

Jimmy takes his pet boa constrictor on a class trip to the farm and creates havoc everywhere.

Chris Van Allsburg. *The Polar Express.* Houghton Mifflin, 1985.

A young boy rides the Polar Express train to the North Pole and is granted his wish: a bell from the reindeer's harness. Although the silver bell slips through a hole in his pocket, he finds it on Christmas morning under the tree.

Judith Viorst. *Alexander and the Terrible, Horrible, No Good, Very Bad Day.* Illustrated by Ray Cruz. Atheneum, 1972.

Alexander wakes up with gum in his hair and doesn't find a prize in the cereal box; these are just the beginning of his very bad day.

Seven and Eight Year Olds

Jeannette Caines. *Daddy.* Illustrated by Ronald Himler. Harper, 1977.

Windy gets "wrinkles in her stomach" waiting for Daddy to come to pick her up on Saturdays after her parents' divorce.

Donald Hall. *Ox-Cart Man.* Illustrated by Barbara Cooney. Viking, 1979.

Life in an early New England family revolved around raising crops and animals, weaving shawls, knitting mittens, and making brooms from birch branches — all to be sold at Portsmouth Market.

Nancy Larrick. *Mice Are Nice.* Illustrated by Ed Young. Philomel, 1990.
Twenty-five poems about mice by well-known poets. See also *Cats Are Cats* by the same collector-illustrator team.

Jack Prelutsky. *The New Kid on the Block.* Illustrated by James Stevenson. Greenwillow, 1984.
Prelutsky pokes fun at people and situations we would like to avoid through his outrageous verse.

Jane Yolen. *Owl Moon.* Illustrated by John Schoenherr. Philomel, 1987.
Yolen's poetic text and Schoenherr's art follow a little girl and her father on a cold moonlit night to search for owls.

Ed Young. *Lon Po Po: A Red-Riding Hood Story from China.* Philomel, 1989.
Mother warns her three girls not to let anyone in the house when she goes to visit their ailing grandmother. The girls use their ingenuity to get rid of the big bad wolf who inevitably comes.

Nine and Ten Year Olds

Natalie Babbitt. *Tuck Everlasting.* Farrar Straus Giroux, 1975.

Ten-year-old Winnie Foster discovers a magic spring whose water gives everlasting life and meets a family that unwittingly drank from it. She faces a choice of whether or not to drink from the spring.

Beverly Cleary. *Dear Mr. Henshaw.* Illustrated by Paul O. Zelinsky. Morrow, 1983.
Leigh Botts writes to an author, Boyd Henshaw, and gradually reveals his deep concerns about his parents' divorce.

Mary James. *Shoebag.* Scholastic, 1990.
In a reverse of Kafka's *The Metamorphosis*, a young cockroach finds himself transformed into a boy, and has to adapt to life at school.

Bette Bao Lord. *In the Year of the Boar and Jackie Robinson.* Illustrated by Marc Simont. Harper, 1984.
In 1947 Shirley Temple Wong immigrates to Brooklyn, New York, from China and must adjust to a new neighborhood, new school, new language, and new customs.

Lois Lowry. *Number the Stars.* Houghton Mifflin, 1989.
Anne Marie helps her Jewish friend and family escape from Nazi occupied Copenhagen during World War II.

Louis Sachar. *There's a Boy in the Girls' Bathroom.* Knopf, 1987.
Bradley is a behavior problem at school but a new school counselor helps him to eventually believe in himself and take charge of his life.

Eleven and Twelve Year Olds

Marion Dane Bauer. *On My Honor.* Clarion, 1986.

Joel agrees to swim in a treacherous river with daredevil Tony despite his word of honor to his father; when Tony drowns Joel must find the courage to face reality and truth.

Virginia Hamilton. *The People Could Fly.* Illustrated by Leo and Diane Dillon. Knopf, 1985.

African American folktales capture the spirit and good humor of an unconquerable group of people.

Katherine Paterson. *Park's Quest.* Lodestar, 1988.

Parkington Waddell Broughton the Fifth searches for his father's name on the Vietnam War Memorial and for secrets his mother refuses to discuss.

Gary Paulsen. *The Winter Room.* Orchard, 1989.

In winter, eleven-year-old Eldon finds that life on the farm changes and allows time for his uncle's storytelling around the fireside.

Elizabeth George Speare. *Sign of the Beaver.* Houghton Mifflin, 1983.

Thirteen-year-old Matt learns from Native American Attean how to survive in the wilderness in the 1700s.

Jerry Spinelli. *Maniac Magee.* Little, Brown, 1990.

Jeffrey Lionel Magee acquires the nickname Maniac as he makes friends racing across a town split along racial lines.

Robert Westall. *Blitzcat*. Scholastic, 1989.
A black cat travels around England looking for her master during World War II and changes the lives of those she meets.